Doctrines of Hatred, Part I: Anti-Semitism

Anatole Leroy-Beaulieu

Translated By Richard Robinson

Sunny Lou Publishing Company
Portland, Oregon, USA
http://www.sunnyloupublishing.com

Publication Date: December 5, 2023

ISBN: 978-1-955392-44-0

# # #

This translation from French is based on the first half of Calmann-Levy, Éditeurs, 3rd edition of *Les Doctrines de haine: l'antisémitisme, l'anti-protestantisme, l'anticléricalisme*, Paris, 1902.

Contents

Contents

Preface

This book is addressed to people with open minds. It runs counter to a good number of prejudices and flatters none of them, which is not going to please a great number of readers.

It deals with questions wherein one is so seldom used to impartiality that one is ill-disposed to tolerate it, and more than one reader will be scandalized by it as if by an offense and a contradiction. I dare say, however, that this volume is everywhere imbued with the same spirit and that I have never written anything that was more cohesive.

The pages that one is about to read are reproduced from conferences that I spoke at, under the same title, at the *École des Hautes Études Sociales*,[1] whose stenography had been taken for the *Semaine Politique et Littéraire*. I have kept myself only to filling them out on certain points and adding some notes. Some of my listeners had remarked to me that anti-Semitism, anti-Protestantism, and anti-clericalism are perhaps not the only doctrines today that by their violence deserve the epithet of doctrines of hatred. Socialism, which glorifies the class struggle, has no less a right to it. It is one of the reasons that I have decided to place at the beginning of these conferences, as an introduction, a study on the great currents of contemporary politics which appeared in part in the *Revue des Revues*, and where I looked into the causes of

---

[1]*École des Hautes Études Sociales*: School for Advanced Social Studies, founded in Paris in 1897 by Dick May.

the recrudescence, amongst us, of sectarianism and intolerance. If I needed for that to go back to the [Dreyfus] Affair which had so shaken France, I was careful to keep myself above the passions that it had unleashed and, far from restoking the hatreds and rancors that our France has only too greatly suffered, I forced myself to mollify them for everyone's common benefit.

The very men whom I will have failed to convince will accord me this justice at least, that during the course of this work I have always been inspired by the spirit of freedom and the feelings of concord and, allow me to add, the spirit of patriotism and the spirit of charity. I have had no other goal than to combat the hatreds that exist among fellow citizens. "If a house be divided against itself, that house cannot stand," says the Gospel.[2] Our France has never had a greater need to be mindful of it.

For me, while working here for the rapprochement of minds and for religious peace, just as elsewhere I strive for the rapprochement of classes and for social peace, I am aware of fulfilling, at one and the same time, my duty both as a Frenchman and as a Christian.

– PARIS, JANUARY 1902.

---

[2]If a house be divided...: Mark 3:25.

Introduction

Sectarianism and Partisanship

Of the origin or recrudescence, among us, of sectarianism and doctrines of hatred. — How the spirit of tolerance and the spirit of freedom seem everywhere on the decline. — Influence of the Dreyfus Affair. — How extreme parties saw in the Dreyfus Affair a means for agitation. — The spirit of faction and the spirit of proscription. — I. Anti-Semitism. — How it was restoked during the Affair. — Its responsibility in the crisis that traverses France. — Causes of its diffusion. — How, aided by the Affair, it cut France in two. — II. Nationalism. — What it owes to the Affair. — Its violence and excesses. — Its polemical processes. — How it too creates categories among the French. — Those who have no fatherland. — Patriotism and nationalism. — III. Socialism. — How it exploited the Affair. — Everything that Socialism took from it. — Reasons for its diffusion and for its ascendant. — The class struggle and appeals to hatred. — IV. Anti-clericalism. — Whence its reawakening. — Repercussion of the Affair and threats of anti-Semitism. — Of the revendication of common law and the fight against sectarianism.

Anti-Semitism, anti-Protestantism, anti-clericalism are three related phenomena which, by their violence and by their appeals to intolerance, merit, all three, equally almost, the epithet of doctrines of hatred. Before undertaking the study of and researching into, in complete honesty, what their origin is, and what their spirit is, how they resemble each other and how they differ, it is fitting to ask whence they come, their recent diffusion, and their new virulence. How did prejudices, passions, fanaticisms, which only recently

seemed if not forever extinguished, at least asleep, –
how did they awaken, brusquely, with a vigor and a
furor unknown until now? For all those who among
the French know how to rise above partisan politics
and above coteries, for all those who have the courage
to be sincere with one another and look resolutely
into their conscience, the response is easy. There is no
need to look very far for the cause of the recrudescence of this sectarianism; it is due to our internal
quarrels over the last few years, it is due to the struggles and intrigues of parties in and around an event
where partisanship is not involved, and to which it
could not be involved without [committing] a crime.

In the midst of all our divisions, there is one
point on which we are all in agreement. France today
is undergoing the most serious crisis it has gone
through since the war and the Commune. Whence
comes it, this crisis, wherein so many old friendships
have been broken in just a few months, and whence
did the partisan passions and sectarian hatreds acquire
a new harshness? From the Dreyfus Affair which has
so lamentably divided the nation. It comes above all
from the fact that, instead of being a painful judiciary
affair for everyone, the anguishing trial has fallen into
the hands of parties who have exploited it in an inverse sense, for the benefit of their interests and their
passions. If France has so greatly suffered from it, if
the country remains deeply divided by it, it is because
the combatants who in this confused melee fought
uniquely for what they believed to be truth and justice
were too few in number, they were too few in number
who made a scruple of not harming anything respectable, having in view only the justification of in-

nocence and the punishment of crime.

How many of our leaders and politicians saw in the Rennes trial merely a dispute between parties, wherein the important thing for them was to triumph, at any price, over one's detested adversaries? It is because of this that the Affair had so quickly grown and become poisoned through factionalism, which pounced on it as on a prey that it did not wish to let go of. A rich prey, in fact, where everything that ought to respect France ended up becoming involved; the army, magistrature, clergy, parliament, president of the Republic, men and institutions, – all were devoured by furious passions with beautiful teeth. Anti-Semites and nationalists, on the one hand, socialists and anti-clerics on the other, threw themselves onto the Affair, making use of the incidents of the trial like murderous weapons, – the ones against the Jews and their allies, against the Protestants and the "Judaics," against "the Masonic and Panamist Republic", – the others against the Jesuits and the "gallooned," against the Church and the top brass, against the "saber and the aspergillum." Appeasement was so difficult because it was in the best interests of the factions who exploited the Affair to prolong the agitation.

Quite another thing is the feeling of men who place the permanent interests of France above party passions and sectarian hatred. If they could have been divided by the Affair, their patriotism never stopped reproving the violence that it provoked and rallying the French to remain united, for love of the common fatherland.

It is not their fault if the winds of hatred that

blew over France revealed, more than ever, divisions
among the French. As in the saddest epochs of our
history, one demands proscriptions; there are entire
categories of Frenchmen whom one wants to put outside the law, under the pretext of public safety. On the
right and on the left, one hears adversaries contesting,
reciprocally, the title of Frenchman, as if in this
France of ours, of stagnant population growth, the
French were too numerous. The engendered hatred
seems to have become the soul of politics and the
bond of parties; it lends a new harshness to our struggles and to our polemics. "Down with them! Off with
their heads!" seems to have become the rallying cry
of the crowds; when one lets out the *vivat*, the accent
that is employed sounds more like a threat to one's
adversaries. Racial hatreds, denominational hatreds,
political hatreds, one sees rising on all sides the "anti"
this and "anti" that which compete in exclusivism and
injustice, in blind fury and inept anger: anti-Semitism,
anti-Protestantism, anti-clericalism, anti-parliamentar-
ianism, anti-militarism, anti-capitalism, – as if patriotism, as if religion and reason themselves, consisted
in damning and proscribing.

Sectarianism and factionalism are everywhere
and vitiate everything. Never perhaps, since the time
of the Revolution, has the free spirit, or rather the
spirit of tolerance, been so low. The same word, freedom, that previously made young hearts beat, hardly
finds an echo anymore and is scorned by the crowds.
Too many lies have been told in its name. The liberal,
the true liberal, he who wants freedom for everyone,
seems a kind of species on the path to extinction. One
freedom alone would appear dear still to the leaders

of opinion: the freedom to insult and the freedom to spread calumny. As for other freedoms, one might say that we have lost the taste for them and the intelligence of them. The very meaning of political freedom has been obliterated; to save it, a number of defenders want to suppress the freedom of religion, freedom of instruction, freedom of association, freedom of charity, as if all freedoms were not interdependent, as if political freedom ought not to be the guarantee of the others and the guardian of all rights.

Some say that the Affair had torn the political parties apart, turned everything upside down, like a violent wind that wrecks everything in its path. If it had, it would have swept away the ancient barriers and thrown down the walls of the old parties and, by freeing us of the servitude of prejudices and the often outdated rancors, by leaving the field open to new associations, it would have rendered France a service. But, if that is the case, only a small number of Frenchmen who think for themselves would have been emancipated from the tyranny of parties and from the superstition of labels. The rest, the majority, it left them more than ever enslaved to the yoke and to the prejudices of partisanship; it only sometimes changed the labels and official stickers. Far from tearing down or everywhere lowering the barriers, it often raised them. It has given the ascendant to violent types in each group because it has everywhere awakened prejudices, stoked passions, inflamed antipathies, so much so that our democracy, and France with it, seem more than ever carried away by a fatal force towards extreme doctrines and positions.

Another phenomenon equally worthy of re-mark is that political parties as such, those with a well-defined program, are losing ground everywhere, even in elective assemblies and parliament. What does this mean for the country and the electoral mass-es? It means that clearly delineated political parties, those having a common faith and a precise program, under the sway of passions stoked by the Affair, tend today to be replaced by confused groups with vague aspirations that overwhelm on all sides the legal arena of politics. It is akin to violent currents and counter-currents on the agitated surface of the country that threaten to sweep everything away with them and that, by bumping and crashing into each other, make waves in all directions. Of these parallel or opposite currents, four principles can be distinguished that flow together, without blending, in two contrary rivers: anti-Semitism and nationalism on one side, an-ti-clericalism and socialism on the other.

As different as they are in their tendencies or in their inspiration, and whatever right they have not to let us confuse them, anti-Semitism and national-ism, anti-clericalism and socialism resemble each oth-er by their methods of propaganda, by the rapture of their polemics, by their concern for freedom and their propensity to proscribe their adversaries, by their in-vocations to hatred and violence. They have almost equally, but in inverse ways, exploited the Affair and, having lived through it for months, breathing new en-ergy into it, they seek to perpetuate its agitation. They enjoy sustaining the exaltation of the crowds, and in their daily demands or agitations they appeal to the antipathies and prejudices of the people, denouncing their adversaries as wicked people or public enemies who are capable of any sort of crime. They tend, almost equally, to make their doctrines into dogmas, and their grievances into articles of faith; and as they represent a kind of religion for their adepts, they have the ardent faith, the burning zeal, of a Church and, too often even, the intolerance and fanaticism of a sect. They hurl, loudly, interdiction on all sides, casting anathema on everything and anything that resists them, going so far sometimes as to excommunicate the lukewarm and the indifferent, repeating, each in its fashion: "there is no salvation except through us!" Each arrogates to itself, in effect, the mission of saving France and, in order to save it, professes that everything is permissible, laws of exception and legal tyranny, riots in the street or forceful coups by the army.

The most diametrically opposed parties seem to accept as well the perilous doctrine of public safety. Each say that they are able to ensure public safety, brusquely, with the aid of a sort of miraculous operation: revision, revolution, or coup d'etat, alone which, if we are to believe them, can make France both safe and sound. Like too many of our physicians today, they vaunt, in every direction, their surgical method. This ill France, worn down by enervating battles, instead of according it some much-needed peace, they claim to want to apply the sword or fire to it, to amputate its limbs, which they say are rotten or gangrene, to rid it of the parasitic cysts that they believe to discover in her. Unfortunately, or perhaps fortunately for her, they do not all agree on the gangrene members that need amputating, nor on the cancerous

tumors that need extirpating; for some, it is the Jew or
the Protestant; for others it is the Jesuit or the congregations; for some it is the foreigners within, and for
others it is the bourgeois capitalist, or it is the officer,
or it is the army. No matter, for the many Frenchmen
among us who are to be proscribed, there are entire
categories of compatriots to place outside the law;
such is, in the eyes of too many of our contemporaries, the urgent task. Love and support one another,
said the patriot as well as the Christian formerly. Hate
and suppress one another, one and all, seems to be the
maxim of too many of our fellow citizens today.
Also, one might say that France is in a state of moral
civil war, the only sort, fortunately, that could tolerate
the gentleness or the softness of our mores.

I.

Of the all the political phenomena that we have seen
in recent years, one of the most saddening is the diffusion of anti-Semitism. We are not among those who
were surprised by it. For a long time ago now, we
have pointed out the causes and the progress of it.
Several good souls were surprised, previously, by the
importance that we seemed to give to the intrusion in
France of that product of Teutonic origin. Recent
events have demonstrated only too well the clairvoy-
ance of our anxieties.

Under the cover of an equivocal nationalism,
anti-Semitism tends to become one of the factors of
politics. It is nationalism, naturally, that has benefited
the most by the Affair. It made it its thing; it had tak-

en responsibility for it, since the beginning, seeing in it only the instrument of agitation and division, without considering the harm that it could cause the country. It took all the hatred and sophistry that it could draw from it, striving hard, from the beginning, to poison it and expand it until the trial of one man became the trial of an entire race, without growing indignant when others permitted themselves to make the same illegitimate generalizations against the top brass and against the armed forces. If France remains lamentably shaken, anti-Semitism was the first to blame. On the violence and excesses of its polemic, on its obstinacy to impute the faults or crimes of individuals to all their coreligionists, on its pretension to equate hatred for the Jew with a love for the army, on its obstinacy to inflame debates and exalt antipathies when patriotism would instead have counseled calm, falls, far and away, the responsibility of the crisis that the country is going through.

Thanks to the Affair, anti-Semitism has become a force, and, like all forces, it finds sycophants. Men and parties who contest power have no shame in extending a hand to it. Nationalists on the one side, royalists on the other, they have no qualms about begging for its good graces. How could the ambitious not draw near to it when, smiling at it, they are applauded simultaneously in the salons and on the street? If one does not always dare to wear its colors openly, one appropriates its jargon, "France for the French." One is not afraid to claim to adhere to its vague social theses, its conventional ethnology, its brief philosophy of the history of the struggle between the races. For, as one knows, anti-Semitism has its philosophy and its scientific theories. In this regard, it is quite modern, this offshoot of the Middle Ages; it sacrifices to the gods and to the century's idols. The resounding theories on race, the struggle for existence, the vital competition that our epoch has so abused, anti-Semitism has appropriated them to itself. If it did not originate with them, it was nourished by it. They have played, for a long time, a part in its fortune. It is the same with this pedantic name of anti-Semitism, imported, with the thing itself, from pedantic Germany. A name with a learned ring to it is a precious thing in these times of religion or scientific superstition. Anti-Semitism, if we are to believe Renan, rested completely on the age-old opposition that existed between the "Semitic" and "Aryan" races which Renan had, in his youth, imprudently made into a sort of law of history. This theory, abandoned by him in his maturity, and fallen out of fashion everywhere, for all the good it did, remains a dogma for our anti-Semites, happy to cloak their hatreds in a sheen of science. For them, the history of the world is merely a duel between the honest Aryan and the vile Semite, so much so that the Rennes trial would be an epilogue to the Battle of Zama and the Battle of Poitiers. But who, other than simple-minded people, can still be persuaded that by crying "Down with the Jews!" a person is continuing in the footsteps of the Scipios, Charles Martel, or Godfrey of Bouillon? The doctors of anti-Semitism themselves, since they made Algeria the land of election, have had to leave their favorite theory behind in Marseille. On crossing the Mediterranean, the anti-Semite, in contact with Arabs and Islam, must take off his pretentious scientific disguise in order to become a common anti-Jew again.

If one wishes to associate it with modern theories of science, anti-Semitism is, in large part, an instance of atavism or a "relic." It is, as one says in Germany, from where it came to us, the *Judenhetze* of the Middle Ages; or also, it is one of those "deadmen talking," which have been described to us not so long ago in such beautiful language,[3] one of those deadmen who were believed to be buried forever, but who cry, who gesticulate, who stir among us and around us. It is a revenant, and how many of these revenants do we see stirring, hurling insults at each other, menacing one another in our poor, troubled France, these revenants of the past! Assuredly, the anti-Semite is not the only one; many others, through Jacobinism and through anti-clericalism, to start with, are hardly, they too, anything more than poorly-interred deadmen, specters escaped from the cemeteries of history, who rise up before us and wander about among us, with their poorly-extinguished passions and their outmoded hatreds. And if the Affair deeply shook us, it is because it reawakened in the French so many dozing deadmen who, reanimated by it, have begun to band together and fight, with ancient furies and rancors, as at the time of the Terror or at the time of the [Catholic] League. Whoever imagined himself forming an opinion about the Rennes trial was merely the unconscious echo of atavistic prejudices. And what is true about the Affair is not the only thing that is true about it; how many times, in our confused disputes, do we need to examine ourselves and pinch ourselves

[3]Original footnote: *The Dead Who Speak* (*Les Morts qui parlent*), a novel by E. M. de Vogüé

to be certain that we are still alive, and that by insulting one another and fighting with one other we are
something else than the spokesperson for the dead
and the hereditary champions of old ancestral battles!

But, in order to be the survivors of the past
that our contemporary politics are still encumbered
by, the anti-Semite is no less nourished by quite living passions and active hatreds, passions that are of
every age and of our democratic age perhaps more
than any other. To be fair, this contemporary anti-
Semitism is a strange and troubling mixture. One
finds everything in it, elevated feelings and noble inspirations, together with vile instincts and brutal passions, warped generosities alongside unbridled appetites. It is this heterogeneous blend of good and
evil, lost idealism and practical materialism, naïve
protestations against the cult of Mammon and unspo-
ken covetousness for riches, indignant revolts against
the prepotency of money and interested rancors or envious jealousies, that anti-Semitism owes its popularity and its diffusion to; for, in this way, it has a double
hold on simple souls, taking them from above and
from below at one and the same time, as by the two
extremities of human nature, so that, noble or vulgar,
our contemporaries have difficulty warding it off. As
if one had the right to make the Jew into the sole author and sole beneficiary of all our ills, there enters
into it, at the same time, a disgust for the villainies of
the day, revolts of conscience against too rapid fortunes, against the corruption of politicians, against the
public display of a provoking pomp, and also the resentments of ousted candidates or unfortunate business men for their more fortunate or more able rivals;

the envy of property owners and lords of manors whose revenues are drying up for the banker and the stock broker whose liquid capital always seems to be growing; aristocratic rancors for new fortunes and new influences, and provincial and rural rancors for the *parvenus* from large cities and the *nouveaux venus* from foreign countries; not to mention the envious malevolence of small shopkeepers and the lower bourgeoisie when faced with department stores, the upper bourgeoisie, and fat capitalists; so much so that one can say that anti-Semitism is a bundle of all the rancors and all the envies further exasperated by the terror of occult influences and dark powers, big banks, and cosmopolite syndicates, vague specters whose invisible hand is thought to be seen everywhere by the ignorant naïvety of the masses. A bundle of envies and a bundle of prejudices as well, – atavistic prejudices, religious prejudices, racial prejudices, economic prejudices, class prejudices, worldly prejudices as well; for, of all the ingredients that enter into the composition of this unhealthy drug, snobism is one of the most frequent among us, and one knows what the power of snobism is in our republic. It is manifested even in the Affair, dictating men's opinion and, even more so, that of women, according to the milieus and circles one frequents. Now, anti-Semitism has made its way into the salons; it is their way, theirs also, of protesting against the insolences of a luxury that they cannot equal, against the arrogant intrusion of the parvenus, against the preponderance of monied people, against even the iniquities of "capitalism" and against "social parasitism."

For the rantings of anti-Semitism against finance and capital lead it to a vague anti-capitalism, arriving at a sort of ingenuous, unconscious, and inconsequent socialism, a socialism, I dare say, of those who do not see where their ideas tend. In that regard, anti-Semitism comes together with socialism; they are like two enemy brothers who have grown up, side by side, in two different environments. From the economic point of view, in effect, anti-Semitism is practically the socialism of the salons, the socialism of the clubman and the country squire, the worldly socialism of all those whose rents are inferior to their appetites or ambitions, the bourgeois socialism of all the vanquished people in life and all those discontent with their fortune. That sort of socialism, without the vain scientific disguise, as well as without the deceiving adornment of the ideal and without the aureole of fraternity; socialism, which has the advantage over the other of attaching itself only to a definite group, imposed from without, so that by railing, with the anti-Semites, against the crimes of monopolizers or the abuses of capitalism, the Parisian bourgeoisie or provincial gentlemen avoid the risk of friendly fire and being the first victims of angers stirred up by their rantings.

That is, it must be said, one of the reasons for the popularity of anti-Semitism. To all the discontented, to all those who place the responsibility for their deceptions or their suffering on others, anti-Semitism furnishes a scapegoat, far easier and reassuring for our egos than the "bourgeois" whom the socialists take on. The bourgeois is a vague being, poorly defined; one knows too well where he comes from; the bourgeois, it's you or me; to get upset with him can be dangerous for you. The Jews, on the other hand, are precise, are limited; they designate a closed group, a manner of caste, just like, during the Revolution, the nobleman or the priest did. By attacking the Jews, by denouncing them to the suspicions and rage of the crowd, the bourgeois does not compromise the anti-Semite's security; he deflects onto someone else the resentments of the masses, all the while satisfying his own rancors or envies. Anti-Semitism is, thus, a way of channeling social hatreds. The error lies in believing that, in our France, strong feelings raised against wealth and capital can be limited to banging on the guichets of the Israelite banks or on the walls of Jewish mansions and that, to shelter oneself from fiscal harassments or mob violence, on the day when people wish to proceed to a "revision of fortunes," it would suffice, as during Holy Russia, to hang a cross or a Virgin on one's door.

The leaders of anti-Semitism are not at all ignorant about this; as much as they might try to resurrect old fanaticisms, they feel that contemporary France, despite everything, remains rebellious to it. Also, in order to be free of this defect of intolerance, so hateful to French generosity, they pretend not to attack the Jewish religion, but the race. They have not stopped repeating it, over the course of the Affair, at the same time that they stoked religious passions, without realizing that race, with the Jews, is inseparable from religion, and that to find fault with race, of distant and doubtful origins, smacks of an anti-Christian hatred and a more serious intolerance; for one can change one's religion, one cannot change one's race. But, be that as it may, it is the blood of Jacob,

not that of Moses, that we must close the doors of our
highest offices to, the magistrature, the administration, the university, all the professions reputed to be
noble; but this blood of the patriarchs, this Semitic
race, by what sign, by what stigmata, shall we recognize it? Will it be, as with the negro, by the color of
the skin? Or would it rather be by the curvature of the
nose? No matter what the Jews' enemies say, the only
recognizable sign of Jewishness is religion; religion is
what preserves it and distinguishes it; to wage war
against the Jew is to pitch battle against the Synagogue; but doing so is to revolt against religious freedom and equality. The laws of exception, claimed
against Judaism, would inevitably have a religious
character to them, and, so that the Jew might not escape our anti-Semites by the means of a deceptive
baptism, as their precursors did in Spain, the anti-
Semite would be forced to establish among us, in the
absence of auto-da-fé, something that the *ancien
régime* of France never tolerated: an Inquisition.

They have understood this rather well, those
French who do not belong to the cult of the majority,
the descendants of those Huguenots, formerly perse-
cuted and pursued, they too in the name of religious
unity, as much to say national unity, for then as now
one tended to confound the one with the other. Without having any more personal sympathies for the Jews
than the Catholics do, French Protestants, insomuch
as a religious minority, have felt menaced by anti-
Semitic intolerance. And how to consider their apprehensions as empty when we can see anti-Protestantism as the result of anti-Semitism, the legitimate
offshoot of the latter, made of analogous passions,

similar prejudices, similar rancors, similar envies? It may be, – for we want to be just towards everyone, even if that means being just towards those who, vis-à-vis their adversaries, make so poor an argument for justice, – it may be that anti-Protestantism, just as anti-Semitism itself, has sometimes been provoked by the imprudence of some Protestants, by their participation in anti-clerical fights, or even by the ascendant of Protestants or Jews in a government visibly defiant of Catholics. It does not cost us anything to recognize that anti-Protestantism and anti-Semitism have been, for a number of Catholics, merely the revenge of anti-Catholic politics and anti-clerical campaigns. For, – and it has been a while since we noted it, – anti-Semitism and anti-clericalism are, in many respects, the product and almost the counterpart of each other. Without anti-clericalism, we would not have had anti-Semitism perhaps, and still less anti-Protestantism.

No less true is the humiliation that we have felt on hearing glorified, publicly, the revocation of the Edict of Nantes, just like the expulsion of the Jews during the Middle Ages. These apologies of great acts of intolerance of the past, formerly timid and as if ashamed, – the Affair has made them bolder and louder. By consequence, it has had the effect of reanimating, with the intolerance of the ones, the apprehensions of the others; it has brought religious minorities closer together, in fearful communities, and as if at war, one passes voluntarily from being defensive to being offensive, and when intolerance begets intolerance, the Affair has, in response, awakened the anti-clerical defiances and the Jacobin hatreds, so much so that, right and left, all the fanaticisms have been overexcited at the same time.

It is in this way that with the help of a trial which religion had nothing to do with, anti-Semitism has come to cut France in two, by a confessional chasm. On one side, the still-believing Catholics, those whom their adversaries call the clericals, with their political or worldly allies; – on the other, the Jews, the Protestants, the free thinkers, those whom the anti-Semites call the "Judaizers"; – and between these two [extremes], suspected by both camps, the Christians who make a scruple of not exiling anyone from Christian charity, or the French who dare to re-gard the Jews as men having the same rights as other men, – unpardonable temerity in the eyes of sectari-ans used to discovering everywhere bought con-sciences, as if they refused to believe in the miracle of disinterested convictions.

And there you have it, by the slow work of an-ti-Semitism, with the help of the Affair, France, which had so much need of religious peace and inter-nal concord, sees itself thrown back, more than ever, under the pretext of national unity, into the sterile conflicts of races and confessions. *Abyssus, abyssum*[4]; anti-Semitism has revived, with anti-clericalism, the instincts of violence and the fury of proscriptions, so much so that to a number of French people it seems that in order to reestablish peace in France the only thing left to do is to designate the victims to be pro-scribed and the freedoms to be sacrificed.

---

[4]*Abyssus abyssum*: Latin for "deep calleth unto deep." Psalm 42:7, KJV.

II.

We will not insult nationalism by confounding it with anti-Semitism. No matter how often, too often, they give each other a hand, their inspiration, in principle at least, is different. Nationalism, for the mass of its adherents, is born of the exaltation and anguishes of patriotism. It is, I will say, exasperated patriotism, sometimes embittered patriotism. Now, even when it would have something morbid about it (and this should be of no surprise for an ill country), patriotism, for those of us who maintain above all else the idea of the fatherland, remains respectable, even in its excesses and its distractions. But, inasmuch as it proceeds from a most noble feeling, a feeling that we are honored to share, it does not follow that nationalism, in the form that it tends to take as a party, is always reassuring for our patriotism. Inasmuch as it appeals to the love of the fatherland, it does not follow that nationalism is not inspired, it too, by the spirit of hatred.

Nationalism is certainly a beautiful name for a party, like a bright-colored standard that floats high over our heads. Nationalism sounds proudly in the ear; but, all things considered, it is as vague as it is sonorous, and I fear that this vagueness even is not foreign to the fortune of the name and the thing. From monarchists to "patriotic socialists," that motley-colored group puts its army on display, lined up under this confusing banner! Nationalism is a new word among us French people, more ancient perhaps and less obscure in literature than in politics. Nationalism is easily understood in a country oppressed by an external master, as is found still, to our shame, in more than one place in Europe, – in Ireland, for example, where the nationalists demand, with Home Rule, a parliament in Dublin. But in our France, can the word have the same meaning? Is France an Ireland or a Poland, deprived of its government and its flag? Is it a conquered country, and does it request, in vain, like Ireland, for a national parliament? If it is oppressed (parties are often oppressive), is it by masters from without, who govern it on behalf of a foreigner? To this question, a number of nationalists do not hesitate to respond in the affirmative. Do all you can to point out to them the Luxembourg and the Palais Bourbon where our legislatures, elected by the nation, sit, they maintain that France is held in servitude, if not by a foreign garrison, at least by foreign agents or accomplices, cosmopolites and "those without a country," among whom figure, naturally, the Jews.

Nationalism and anti-Semitism cross paths here. To hear them speak, France does not belong to itself; despite all the powers it possesses, directly or indirectly, from popular election, France is subject to tyrants, which would not be the first time in its history perhaps; but what it has never tolerated is that these tyrants are the henchmen of a foreigner. France is, for many years, under the government of a syndicate of country-less citizens who, although inscribed in our state registers, are not, for all that, French; and this shameful yoke, – the French, the true French, have the right and the duty to break it.

And there you have it, in all its excess, the

thesis that is presented to us, each morning, in a portion of the French press. It is new for us; it goes back only a small number of years; it only assumed its full strength and its complete popularity during the Affair and because of the Affair. Its scope is felt: it tends to nothing less than the creation of categories among the French, according to the ones in order to refuse to the others that fine name of Frenchman, our common patrimony, imitating in that the anti-Semites and, like the anti-Semites, acting, under the pretext of national unity, cutting the country in two, arbitrarily excommunicating a portion of French citizens from French nationality.

A national policy, as the nationalists promise us, would be, it seems, what would work to reestablish the harmony and union of the French, to bring closer, in the same feeling of tolerance and patriotism, all the children of the same country, without distinction of origin, religion, party.

This policy of national reconciliation, is it really what the loudest organs of nationalism are advocating?

To the words of peace, too many prefer the cries of hatred and the threats of war. The national peace that they let us hope for, it seems to expect nothing short of crushing those whom they call the "bad French." At a time that France would have need, more than ever, of a policy of appeasement in the style of Henri IV, the majority of nationalists obstinately continue to throw anathema at their adversaries, placing them under interdiction, like enemies of the fatherland. For too many of them, patriotism

appears to consist in denying others the quality of being French. This title of Frenchman which character-
izes us, whatever our political or religious opinions
might be, they assume the privilege and as if the monopoly of it. To believe the most exalted among them,
the French, the true Frenchman would be a minority
in France. We heard, in the High Court, with little or
no surprise almost, a nationalist, as a witness on the
stand, say of the accused: "He is a Frenchman, which
has become quite rare."

   Is it with such a spirit of exclusivity that the
ingenuous patriots imagine fortifying the national
feeling? They are not afraid to distinguish, on French
soil, two categories of inhabitants whom they put in
opposition to each other: the true French, the Frenchmen of France – and the others, the false ones, the
pseudo-French, French foreigners or domestic foreigners, a damning opposition that would be tantamount to civil war. When I hear certain discourses, I
am reminded, in spite of myself, of those naïve paint-
ings of the Last Judgment where archangels with a
sword in hand separate men into two flocks, the good
and the bad, the sheep and the goats,[5] the blessed and
the damned. If we have seen something similar in other epochs, during the Revolution notably, France was
at war then, and in the ranks of foreign armies were
emigrants who bore arms against her. Do we not see
something similar today? To cut France in two, in the
name of national sentiment which ought to be the
binding element, to deny to our political adversaries
the title of Frenchman in order to excite against them

---

[5]Last Judgment... the sheep and the goats...: See Matthew
25:31-46.

the suspicions of the masses and the hatred of simple folk, is not only to pour poison into the open wounds of France caused by partisanship, it is to commit a sin against the fatherland, by falsifying the notion of pa- triotism.

Like anti-Semitism, by which it is too often inspired, nationalism has thus become, it too, for too many of its adepts, a doctrine of hatred. Formerly – and its detractors have reproached it considerably on this score – the most exalted patriotism, or the coars- est form of it, which was withered by applying the so- briquet of chauvinism to it, believed it could be forti- fied by fomenting prejudices and hatred against for- eigners; today, it is no longer only against foreigners that nationalism, which presents itself to us as the cer- tified representative of patriotism, excites the defi- ance and aversion of the masses, it is against fellow citizens, against the French, against those whom it is not afraid to call domestic enemies. It does in no way realize that under the pretext of defending integrity it risks tearing up by its own hands the unsewn tunic of French unity.

Among all the great powers of Europe, France had a privilege, which was numbering, at home, only its children, happy to be a part of it. It had neither a Poland, nor an Ireland, and that was its strength. We were proud, for good reason, to be all French in France. This privilege, would we have lost it, or would we deprive ourselves of it? Parties have the mania of becoming purified; it is an operation that rarely succeeds. It is also dangerous for a people. To become purified is often to become weak; what would that be like for a country like France with a stagnant population?

A nation is not a Church; it does not have the right to excommunicate its members or to chase out heretics from its bosom in the name of I do not know what dogma or what orthodoxy. But that is what many nationalists have come to. They speak, they judge, they reprove, they anathematize, in their reunions, like Church Fathers at a council. They have for a maxim: "No French except for our own." They tend to create categories of suspects among us whom they designate to the people as the authors of all our ills, and they do that under a form that excites popular angers the most, as the avowed or secret instruments of the foreigner. And among these traitors in the pay of the enemy, or among their accomplices, many do not hesitate to include the men currently in power, to begin with the head of State, and each morning they incite the country to deliver itself from this humiliating yoke. But by what means? – by all means, the majority of nationalists having come to the point of resorting to force, to a coup d'état, to insurrection in the street, or a military rebellion. Against foreigners, in fact, and against traitors in their service, anything is legitimate. How to have scruples about legality when it is a matter of restoring independence and honor to France?

The first thing to do, the urgent work, we are told, is to deliver the country of the syndicate of cosmopolites and the country-less who oppress it; that done, the French will begin to get along with each other. That really does seem like the slogan, if not the program, of the nationalists in broad strokes, in agreement with the anti-Semites.

The Affair gave them that, for nationalism owes a great deal to the Affair; if it did not originate with the Affair, it is nourished by it and it has lived by it. The cosmopolites, the country-less, I will not say, with the skeptics, that it is an imaginary race that exists only in the elucubrations of ill minds. Alas, no! even if they were merely a vile and turbulent minority in France, the country-less are not a myth that was invented by nationalism for the needs of the cause. If they further its agenda, they does so, as is often the case, without wishing to or without realizing it, by ignorance or by fanaticism. The country-less, – excuse me for bringing it up, – we have personally run into them, on multiple occasions, in the last few years, at public reunions that we organized, my friends and I, for youth at schools. There, in the Latin quarter, doubtless because we put the word "fatherland" front and center in our motto,[6] we have often been obstinately interrupted by cries of "Down with the fatherland!" which French ears could never grow accustomed to.[7]

These blasphemies against the fatherland mixed with cries of "Long live anarchy!" – where do they come from? Are they from the mouths of

[6]Original footnote: *Patrie, Devoir, Liberté* [French for "Fatherland, Duty, Freedom"], the motto of the "Committee for the Defense and Social Progress."

[7]Original footnote: See the Conferences of the "Committee for the Defense and Social Progress" whose stenographic minutes have been published by the *Réforme sociale* and reproduced in propaganda brochures.

deputies or senators, men of power or magistrates? No, they come from the little people, often wet behind the ears, who, by having outraged in this way what is most sacred in French hearts, imagined in their naïve cynicism to give proof of free spirits and strong spirits. If nationalists limited their anger to these insulters of the fatherland, whether anarchists or collectivists, we would stand with them in solidarity, and all of France would march behind them. But if there are, in the seediest quarters of our large cities, those who have gone-astray and who make a profession of renouncing the fatherland, is he a patriot to falsely swell the ranks and to proclaim before Europe that France is in their hands? Of all the cries let out in the street or in public halls, at a time when political parties so willfully vociferated outrages of every sort against all things and all peoples, unscrupulously insulting all institutions and all high offices, as if respect and courtesy were old-fashioned superstitions to us, – the cries of "Down with the fatherland!" and the even those of "Down with the army!" are even rarer from those in whom they find, fortunately, the least echo. What right do we have to attribute them unjustly to men who often do not reprove those cries any less than we do? Or, what amounts to the same thing, what right do we have to treat them as cosmopolites and men without a country, those who permit themselves other ideas than we have on the role of the State and on the constitution of public powers? Or those even who have a different opinion than we do on the military process or on the political process?

The feeling for the fatherland is still alive, thank God, in all the ranks, in all the classes. The Affair itself has shown us its susceptibilities and vigor. National sentiment remains so alive that it is enough merely to mention the fatherland in order to make the country vibrate. Nationalism has understood this, and from this it derives its strength. To rally a large part of the public opinion behind it, it need only show how patriotism is put at risk by cosmopolitanism. The majority of nationalists have done that in good faith, of course; but it would be unnecessary, in overexciting patriotism against the so-called cosmopolites, that they should appear to make an instrument of power out of it and, let's not mince words, an electoral advertisement.

Patriotism is not the monopoly of any party, and as soon as it is built into a party nationalism has no right to lump all its adversaries under the vague name of cosmopolites.

The reproach of cosmopolitanism, internationalism, is something that patriots ought to employ with the greatest scruple; it is poorly defined; it is ambiguous and, like the accusation of forming a State within a State, it can often turn against the imprudent sorts who take advantage of it. It is one of the grievances of anti-clericalism, as it is one of the grievances of anti-Semitism. It is one of those that factions and sects hurl at each other most voluntarily. It has been launched, in turn, against the most diverse parties, against almost all the religious and political groups, against the Jews, against the Protestants, against the Catholics and congregations, against Freemasons and against socialists, so much so that all men whose religious faith or social expectations surpass the strict

limits of the fatherland, all those who have coreligionists abroad, would be more or less affected by it.
By this reckoning, the majority of French people
would be cosmopolites.

One must not however, under the pretext of
patriotism, intend to cloister us, to wall us in within
our mutilated frontiers, forbidding us all communion
of beliefs, ideas, or sentiments with the outside. This
would be to shrink the intellectual and national hori-
zon of France, and to clip the wings of our national
genius which, in all periods, has hovered at great dis-
tances above the world. To be French, we are not
forced to excommunicate ourselves from humanity;
that would be, on the contrary, a manner of being unfaithful to the French ideal. Every religion has its superstitions that spoil it; and it is true of the religion of
the fatherland as it is of any other; it takes on a nar-
row-mindedness among certain of its devotees, a sort
of bigotry designed to disgust more than to inspire
love. It is one of the reasons for which we hear the fatherland sometimes blasphemed, as others blaspheme
the name of God. If they want to erect the cult of the
fatherland, it is important for nationalists to be on
guard against such excesses; – or would it really be
true that, for the common folk, there can be no religion without superstition or fanaticism?

When, instead of staying above the fray of
politics, religion lowers itself to get involved, it
strongly risks diminishing itself. Perhaps the apostles
of nationalism too easily forget this peril when they
strive to form themselves into a party. Our patriotism's anxieties forbid us to silence them. It does not

seem that by its methods of polemic, or by its contacts with anti-Semitism and anti-Protestantism, nationalism has augmented the cohesion, the security, or the esteem of France.

Not so very long ago we loved to hear it said that every foreigner has two fatherlands, his own and France's. Will nationalism allows us that again? The Affair has furnished it with the occasion to represent France as the object of hatred among peoples. It is to ourselves, to this noble and generous France, if we must believe the nationalist newspapers, that we need to apply the Roman historian's words: *odium generis humani.*[8] At the moment that we are convoking the world to our Universal Exposition, was it really in the service of the dignity or interests of France? In the ardor of their passion, too many nationalists had no qualms about being, as failures of our politics, a party weapon, so much so that they have merited being treated as exploiters of national humiliations. The language of those who present themselves as their leaders is not designed to reassure us; we would want it to be more prudent; but in external affairs, as in internal politics, they tax the prudence of pusillanimity; certain among them would have us pushed voluntarily into simultaneous adventures on land and on sea. Instead of teaching people some tact, sangfroid, self-possession, which alone permit nations a rich and well-adhered to politic, they encourage what has all too often and too many times been fatal to us: deceptive illusions and empty manifestations. One finds, too frequently, among them, boulevardiers who for-

[8]*Odius generis humani*: Latin for "hatred for humanity." *Annales*, 15.44, Tacitus.

merly placed their patriotism as a barrier to the entrance of the Opera for the performance of *Lohengrin*. If they have preconized the Russian alliance, they misunderstood, yesterday even, its pacific character, just as when M. Déroulède, traveling through Russia, boasted about having led it, after us, into a war of revenge. Blind perhaps to subsequent perils, they seem to fail to see that France cannot expose itself, at one and the same time, to the double enmity of Germany and England, and that if it wants to stand up to one of them in the world, it will need to be reconciled with the other in Europe. And there you have it, seemingly, plenty of reasons whereby a friend of freedom and peace might defy plebiscitary nationalists. As excellent as their intentions might be, France, in their hands, would no longer be secure, within or without. Their politics seem to us, at one and the same time, too exclusive and too confused in their aims, too sectarian and too revolutionary in their procedures, too motley in their personnel and too equivocal in their alliances, too untidy finally, too provocative and temerarious with respect to foreigners, to be the instrument of a national recovery. To our great regret, we need to see in that a danger rather than a hope.

For all its claims to strengthen France by restoring its unity, nationalism is instead, for us, a threat and a weakness. The reason is simple; by its violence and by its anathemas, by its appeals to prejudices and to hatred, nationalism has betrayed its name and its program, to such a point that I would dare say that, if patriotism unites us, nationalism divides us.

III.

Just like nationalism, and even more so than nationalism, socialism has made itself, among us, an agent of hatred, at the same time as an instrument of division. Far from feeling ashamed to appeal to the desires and the appetites of the demos, far from disengaging from the grosser economic materialism, it persists in exploiting the rancors and envy of the masses, and with the politics of the class struggle it has raised hatred to the level of a principle.

One could say of socialism that it has two faces, depending on how it looks at the worker or the employer, the proletariat or the bourgeoisie. To the one, it acts as the representative of love and brotherhood; to the other, it appears like the personification of envy and social hatreds. Or, what comes to the same thing, one could say about contemporary socialism that it is born two opposing feelings: if its father is love, hatred is its mother. It takes unequally after these two parents, whose rival influence fights in it nonstop; if, in its infancy, it appeared to be rather inspired by its father, it tends, on getting older, to take its mother's advice primarily. It is always the case that in its propaganda it shows more faith in the strength of hatred than in that of love and brotherhood.

Socialism tends, what is more, it too, to assume the aspect and the spirit of a sect – and a sect that erects altars to Hatred and Terror. Also, without insulting it by putting it on the same level as anti-Semitism, we are obliged to make room for it beside the doctrines of hatred.

If it was not born of the Affair, if it surpasses it in particular by its pretensions and by its aspirations, socialism was, it too, nourished by it and animated by it for many months. It exploited it, just as anti-Semitism and just as nationalism did, although in reverse. While the latter presented itself as the sole representative of the idea of the fatherland, socialism affected to call itself the sole defender of the idea of justice, as if these two great things, Patriotism and Justice, could be separate in a country like France, or as if patriotism did not refuse to tolerate such a divorce.

Any more than the idea of a fatherland, the idea of justice is not the monopoly of any one party. In vain do the socialists try to corner the market on it, in the eyes of youth or those of the masses. It is not that we doubt their good faith or their love for justice. We do not doubt the sincerity of anyone, socialists and nationalists, adversaries or not. We believe that it is to ill-serve France to treat as criminals or traitors those who do not think like us. What we reproach socialists for is not for constantly having the word justice on their lips, even though we do not always understand this word in the same way as they do; it is for having exploited this idea of justice and for having monopolized it, just as the nationalists did with the idea of fatherland; it is for having pretended, they too, to convert the Affair, which divided us, into an instrument of their party, to the point of presenting themselves to us as the sole defenders of the Republic and of the Law. Inadmissible pretension for Frenchmen who are still concerned about the freedom and prosperity of France. For, while the socialists would have wished to pass themselves off as the sole champions of Law and Justice, something that the facts do not allow us to concede, that would not prove the verity of socialism, nor the well-foundedness of its theses regarding the State, family, inheritance, property. These important social matters have nothing to do with the Rennes trial. They would be unable to be decided on by sympathies or antipathies. Socialists can, in the eyes of the nation, drape themselves all they want in the mantle of Justice, their doctrines are neither more certain nor less dangerous.

This is a truth that must be kept in mind, for many around us seem to be unaware of it. It establishes, in socialism's favor, a confusion between its vague aspirations for justice and its economic and political theories. This is, in large part, what gives it its strength. Whence comes, in fact, let's be honest, its ascendant over the masses and over so many noble spirits? Is it uniquely from its appeal to appetites, hunger, envy, hatred? Assuredly not; its growing strength comes from the fact that, instead of always addressing vile and violent instincts, it invokes, at the same time, with resounding violence, generous ideas, high aspirations, which are too often forgotten or railed against by our materialistic age, these ideas of Christian origin which are the honor of our civilization and which, despite all sacrilegious pretensions, forever maintain a hold on our youthful souls, as on the populace's soul; ideas of justice, brotherhood, solidarity among men and among nations. Socialism knew how to attract to itself some striking and noble patronesses, and one understands that they owe their proselytes to those who act and appear in their name.

In a word, and in total opposition to the politics on the
ground which is uniquely preoccupied with interests,
socialism brings an ideal to the people, so much so
that one could present it as a sign of the renaissance
of idealism, although, on the other hand, one could
find in it the product of the philosophical materialism
of the century and of the gross positivism of the masses.

In any case, by virtue of this invocation to the
ideal, modulated in melodious variations by able vir-
tuosos, like a call from on high to the gates of a new
Eden, the fact is that socialism, like a popular Or-
pheus playing on an enchanting lyre, solicits a great
many young enthusiasms and summons a large number of good hearts who follow behind it, in addition
even to the masses who expect power and well-being
from it. As for myself, I would forgive it a great deal,
without, for all that, believing any more in its dogmas, if its adepts were always faithful to this high ideal; if they remained, even in their chimeras, knights of
Justice and missionaries of Brotherhood; if they com-
batted primarily in order to heal the soul or the body
of the people of its moral maladies or its physical bur-
dens, in order to free its conscience from the servitude
of degrading vices; if, like the first Christians whom it
had no qualms to let itself be compared with, they really brought to our world, which is older than and
perhaps as ill as the Roman world was, a gospel of
peace and love.

But is it really what they do, in truth, in their
epistles to their brothers, or in the solemnity of their
national or international councils, these apostles of

this new religion that pretends, in turn, to change the face of the world? Like other evangelists, whom humanity has blessed the advent of, are they not, they too, unfaithful to their ideal and, under the cover of brotherly love, is it not envy, rancor, and hatred that they go habitually preaching to the masses who are assembled around them? Does not class warfare remain the last word of their catechism? The fathers of their Church, have they not proclaimed it in their last synods? In order to hear what the dogma of class warfare makes of the doctrine of brotherhood, one need only let the socialists intone in choir their celebratory songs. We have heard them, those hymns of the new Church, the *Carmagnole*, the *Ça ira*, and *Les Bourgeois on les pendra!*[9] And there you have them, the psalms and canticles of the socialist liturgy; there you have it, in the manner in which it is expressed, at the end of their brotherly feast, the humanitarian idealism of the new prophets. After that, how to be scandalized if there are still some good souls who in these revolutionary refrains prefer "the old song" and the antique act of charity of the ancient faith?

Socialism has the legitimate ambition of becoming a great party, and to judge by the number of its adherents, the zeal of its proselytes and the intelligence of its leaders, it has already arrived; why does it not sever itself from the coarseness of the street and the pranks of the estaminet? Socialism aspires to present itself as a government party, and no one can

---

[9]*Carmagnole,* the *Ça ira*...: French songs from the time of the French Revolution. *Les Bourgeois on les pendra* is a modified lyric from *Ça ira;* it means "The Bourgeoisie will be hanged." (In the original the words are "The aristocrats will be hanged.")

defy it anymore to succeed because several of its leaders have entered into the ministry and the socialist group has shown itself to be, in the Chamber, the firmest supporter of the Waldeck-Rousseau Cabinet. Since then, why does it not abandon, in Palais-Bourbon, the indecent vociferations and boisterous methods of oppositions lacking in numerical force or lacking in moral authority, which can expect nothing but deafening noise and scandal? Why does it not have the courage to break off with the violence and the violent sorts, and why does it not dare to repudiate the savage propaganda and barbarous attempts by the proponents of anarchy? Socialism, finally, includes today in its ranks a large number of "intellectuals" originally from the bourgeoisie; it welcomes, with open arms, all the young people who come to it, from the student benches of the University or higher education; by what contradiction does it obstinately insist on making the class struggle the cornerstone of its program and its politics? Would it be that, in all the parties, the direction must rest with the violent sorts, and that, of all the appeals to human reason, the appeal to hatred is still the best understood?

Class warfare remains the order of the day among socialists. The social transformation that they promise us, they persist to seek it, not in the conciliation of rights and in the union of hearts, but in the antagonism of the employer and the employee and in the clash of interests. The Jerusalem of their dreams, their future brotherly city, they entrust its erection to hatred. If they protest against militarism, if they invite us to enjoy peace and love with others, it is only to enlist citizens of the same country against each other.

For national rivalries, for conflicts between peoples, however intermittent they might be, they threaten to substitute an everyday internecine war among the French. These fervent apostles of human solidarity end up, like the anti-Semites, preaching division and war. For the devotion to the fatherland, for national solidarity, a number of them pretend to substitute a new class or caste spirit, which they call workers' solidarity or international proletarian solidarity. But who could say this was progress? The class or caste spirit, whether that be of the nobility, the bourgeoisie, or the working class, is narrow and selfish; it tends to make the interests of one fraction of society predominate over the general interests of the country; it is fatally limited, exclusive, tyrannical; it leads everywhere to hatred and conflict. Whereas patriotism is a principle of union, the hatred among classes is a principle of division. Whereas love for the fatherland is a bond between all the inhabitants of the same soil, class jealousy is a cause for egoism and disunion. Through it, France and humanity would be cut into hostile layers, into inimical and irreconcilable slices.

Just like the anti-Semites, the socialists create, they too, categories among the French, striving to fit those whom they call the workers into a firm caste, excluding thousands of Frenchmen from their socialist France, not only under the pretext of religion or race, but, what amounts to the same thing, under the pretext of class or profession; arranging men into two camps, according to the cut of their suit or the shape of their hat; demanding the monopoly of power for manual laborers; brushing aside, except in inconsequential cases like the friends or henchmen of the detested bourgeoisie, all those with soft, uncalloused hands, without appearing to notice that among the bourgeoisie they excommunicate the majority of the French who have made the glory and the strength of France.

To be sure, the largest part of our socialists act in good faith (except for those, at least, who proclaim themselves internationalists), when they reject, like an undeserved insult, the epithet of "countryless"; but if they remain patriots, or if they convince themselves that they are, the majority of them fail to recognize the existing conditions of modern nations. Carried away by the logic of their principle, or blinded by the mirages of their chimeras, they fail to see that Europe remains, alas! a camp where only the strong have the right to live. Just as they form a class or caste party, they are inclined to subordinate national interest to class interests. Socialism boasts about having taken the place of religion in the heart of the people, but this social religion which, it too, has its fanatics, has no fear of putting dogmas or superstitions above the idea of the fatherland. Whence, whether conscious of it or not, socialism tends to diminish or deform national feeling, while justifying, unawares, the reproaches made by nationalists or anti-Semites. It makes no scruple, in its annual congresses, of raising a flag against a flag, as if to the noble banner of France it preferred the red banner of the international proletariat. It is not afraid to offend the legitimate susceptibilities of patriotic sentiment and, each time the Russian Tsar has paid a visit to the Republic, the socialists aren't ashamed to unleash their outrage on the guests of France, at the risk of making every alliance and ev-

ery foreign policy impossible. They persist in showing their little concern for French power, seemingly
unable even to understand that in order to be free a
modern democracy needs to be strong. What is more,
in its haste to seize power, for the benefit of what it
calls the Fourth Estate, socialism attacks, simultaneously, all the institutions that have made France
strong, as if it could only rule over ruins.

The army, the organized national force, the
army having remained, despite everything, the ram-
part of our independence, seems to have become the
enemy of our socialists, as if the era of universal
peace had already been raised over the world. This
was quite evident during the Affair. If, after hesita-
tions that they were unable to erase all trace of, the
bulk of socialists had thrown its weight behind the
side opposed to the Chiefs of Staff, it has not at all always done so out of pure love for truth or justice. It is
because they saw there a means to disparage the army
and to discredit the military spirit, imputing the fault
of some of them, audaciously, to all its leaders; attributing, it too, to the army, not in order to justify it,
but to condemn it, the iniquitous theory of the bloc.
Socialism seems, as a result, to have become synonymous with anti-militarism; and so manifest has the
passion of collectivist newspapers become against the
army that it has singularly diminished the range of
their most eloquent pleas in favor of justice. By these
same excesses of its polemic, by its coarse and low
insults at anyone who wears the epaulette, by the
hateful propaganda directed at the casernes, socialism
has driven nationalists and anti-Semites to excess, in
the opposite direction. It has been, in spite of itself,

one of the principle instigators of nationalism, for it
has revolted our national instinct which feels, confus-
edly, that in Europe and in the Triple Alliance, France
cannot exist without an army and that the army cannot exist without discipline and without a military
spirit.

Socialism is obstinate in its refusal to recognize this truth, and when its principle would constrain
it to, we do not know how we could pardon it. Of
course, many things stand between us; we cannot accept its utopias, nor its sophisms, nor its declama-
tions, nor its violence; we are unable to tolerate the
equivocations of its propaganda, and we must unmask
the double face under which it presents itself to both
workers and countryfolk successively. We are unable,
above all, to allow it to poison people's suffering or
embitter people's soul by piling, each day, rancors
and hatred on its head. But even if it did not manifest
to us its disdain for individual liberties and its scant
regard for the rights of conscience and family; even if
it did not put private property or public wealth at risk,
and if it did not threaten us with universal impover-
ishment which the little people and the most humble
among us would have been the first victims of; if we
did not hold against it neither economic grievances,
nor moral grievances, we would still have to defend
against socialism's attacks on the essential organs of
French power, not to mention social peace and the co-
hesiveness of the fatherland; and that alone would
force us to regard socialism as a danger for the greatness and for the independence even of France.

IV.

There is another party or, if one prefers, another doctrine, that often allies with socialism and which, to
free spirits, inspires even more repugnance, a completely negative party made of inveterate prejudices,
of Jacobin authoritarianism and sectarian hatreds, the
entirety of it covered by a false varnish of liberalism
and equipped with a defrocked scientific pedantry.
You guessed it right: we are talking about anti-clericalism.

If it had no other aim than to defend the
sovereignty of the State and the independence of civil
society against outdated pretensions, we would not be
the last to join with it in fighting the lingering adversaries of political freedom or freedom of thought. But
the efforts of anti-clericalism today, among the majority of its adepts, is not limited to that. For most of
them, the word "clerical" has become synonymous
with Catholic; every man who is faithful to the old
Church is a secret or outright adversary who must be
held in suspicion and who deserves being passed over
for any public office. Instead of an instrument of
emancipation, anti-clericalism has shown itself to be
an agent of discord and oppression. What is more, anti-clericalism, among a number of its adherents, itself
carried away by a fanatic zeal, goes on the attack after
every vestige of the Christian idea, every trace of a
religious sentiment, the very notion of God, not to
mention the clergy and the Church, as if it were going
after dangerous and immoral superstitions that the
State must strive to uproot. Anti-clericalism ends up
thus becoming a sort of regained clericalism, animat-

ed, it too, by a sectarian spirit, intolerant of others' beliefs and desirous, in its turn, to employ public authority and the ascendant of power against them. This sectarian anti-clericalism, unfaithful to the ideas of tolerance which it pretends to embody, the liberals, having remained respectful of others' freedom and conscience, are constrained to repulse it because, instead of a defender of the freedom of thought, they are compelled to see in it an adversary of religious freedom and an agent of hatred and discord.

If it does not constitute, strictly speaking, a party, anti-clericalism is the soul or the principle of radicalism. It is the habitual bond of republican concentration, a bond made up of common antipathies and enmities, rather than common convictions. Opportunists and radicals, socialists come together in their hatred of the soutane and fear of the wimple.

This anti-clericalism, pretentious and vulgar at the same time, a favorite weapon of politicians in a pickle, naïve adepts present it to us as the next emancipator of French intelligence and the founder of future freedom, as the only or best guarantor of national unity. These promises, these facts, and these acts have shown us what they deserve. To see it at work, militant anti-clericalism hardly proceeds any differently than anti-Semitism; they are nothing but the counterpart and the companion of sorts of each other. Both have voluntary recourse to the same methods of propaganda or polemic, unafraid of appealing to the prejudices and the passions of the masses, not shrinking from calumnious insinuations and deceitful legends; exaggerating, out of proportion, the strength or the fortune of their real or imaginary adversaries; asking for nothing less from them than confiscation and proscription. With the same infantile or simulated terrors, they both look for occult causes in events, pointing out everywhere the hand of mysterious specters, the one discovering the Jesuit's white collar everywhere, the other perceiving the Jew's money everywhere. Just like the anti-Semite, the anti-clerical pretends to liberate French soil from foreign domination and to reestablish, amongst us, the moral unity of the nation; and just like the anti-Semite, it begins to draw up categories of Frenchmen, it is not ashamed to cut France in two, using its two hands to tear up that national unity which it pretends to establish. Similarly, anti-clericalism promises to establish, forever, the reign of freedom and, in order to prepare the foundations for it, it hastens to suppress the freedom of education and of association. It announces religious peace through the neutrality of the State and, under the pretext of establishing peace, it precipitates us into confessional quarrels.

Why these contradictions among doctrines and acts? It is because, for the most ardent of its adepts, anti-clericalism is nothing but a tool of domination, unless it is a sectarian way of acting. The anti-clerical, in effect, is often nothing more than a clerical in reverse, whose iconoclastic zeal intends to tear down God and Christ from their trembling altars in order to replace them by Reason and Humanity. In these revolts against the old faith, it evinces a striking intolerance and an arrogant proselytism, haughtily dogmatizing, as if from the portico of the temples of Science it was speaking truly in the name of infallible

Reason.

How to be surprised that this sectarian anti-clericalism carries everywhere around with it, in politics, the sectarian mindset, too often rendering itself guilty of what it bitterly reproaches the clerics of? It does not hesitate to put the interests of free thought, what it calls the secular interests of Reason and Science, above national interests. It does not oppose it in the least for becoming, in this regard, the accomplice of our adversaries or our rivals, provided that it have a chance to play a dirty trick on a soutane or a tricorne.[10] Do we not hear it, each year, demanding, with an ignorant infatuation, the recall of our ambassador to the Vatican, the abandonment of our religious protectorate, the dispersion of Congregations and Missions, the closure of their schools and their novitiates? Little does it matter that in the Middle East, in Asia, in Africa, in all the world, the missionaries and religious of every stripe are the principals and often the sole propagators of French language and influence! Its hatred of the Church is stronger than its love of France. Compared to the interests of laicization, what does the role of France matter in the world, to the anti-clerical? His only concern is the triumph of new dogma and the ruin of the Church.

This hateful anti-clericalism, the shame of truly free spirits, was on the decline several years ago; to France's and the Republic's honor, it appeared old, demoded, outdated. Leo XIII's broad politics seemed to have taken away its strength, if not its virulence.

---

[10]Soutane or a tricorne: scil. someone belonging to the clergy or the army.

How did it suddenly grow reanimated, more menacing than ever? How is it that the intelligent initiative of the great pope did not produce more abundant and long-lasting effects? Because, and this bears mentioning, anti-clericalism was suddenly revived, it too, during the Affair. It made a pretext of the virulence of some so-called religious newspapers and the fits of rage of a so-called Catholic anti-Semitism to identify the clergy with the ignominies of anti-Semitism and to raise, against congregations and the Church, measures of national defense, analogous to those demanded by anti-Semites against the Jews and the Synagogue. Forget that throughout the entire process of the Affair, it was difficult to discover the clergy's meddling; nevertheless, the Fathers were accused of having arranged everything behind the scenes. That is the traditional manner of operation for the anti-clerical. Suspicious minds, filled with old legends of "the Congregation," have discovered the invisible hand of the Jesuits in the incidents of the Affair. For it is well worth repeating, to our own consternation, that the anti-clerical party reasons in exactly the same way as the anti-Semite; it sees, it too, occult influences and secret motives everywhere. The difference is that the latter attributes everything to the corruptive genius of Israel, while the former blames everything on the spirit of intrigue and domination of Loyola. If one were to believe them, the Jew and the Jesuit would be the two great actors, or rather the secret protagonists, of the great drama of history, given all the strings they pull. They are, in any case, our contemporaries' two scapegoats; they are accused, with almost identical maledictions, by common folk, of all the shames and all the ills of France. The fact is that the anti-Jew and anti-Jesuit are two visionaries, equally affected by a suspicious monomania, analogous to the madness of the persecutions which see in everything a secret and omnipotent enemy, against which their furious delirium enjoins France imperiously to be on its guard. And it is naturally by measures of proscription and laws of exception that both these victims of hallucinations claim to be protecting the country.

The anti-Jew and anti-Jesuit, these two maniacs are exalted, reciprocally, by their mutual extravagances. It is in this way that anti-Semitism plays a large role in the recrudescence of anti-clericalism. One asks, with a certain sadness, how the conciliatory politics of Leo XIII and the pope's advances to the Republic have not assured a better religious peace. The fault is not solely with the prejudices or intolerance of our modern Jacobins, or with a distrustful skepticism of our government leaders; the fault is as much due to anxieties and angers provoked by the fanatic crusade waged by the anti-Semites. For as much as the episcopacy and the high clergy have tried to sidestep the issue, they have exploited their silence in order to make them complicit. The anti-Semite and the anti-Protestant's claim, almost avowed, of making religious unity, on the sill of the 20th century, the sign and the condition of national unity, has been turned against the Catholics. National unity, the moral unity of the nation, which temerarious friends dreamt of remaking to the advantage of the Church, its adversaries have claimed to make it against the Church and to the advantage of free thinkers and anti-clerical societies. It is something that one does not touch with

impunity in a country troubled as our own, the old fanaticisms and the confessional hatreds. Intolerance in-
vites more intolerance and, as we have shown for a
long time now,[11] anti-Semitism and anti-clericalism
tend to stoke and reinforce each other, reciprocally.
They are, in this regard, the product as much as the
collaborator of each other. If we have seen, with a
new animosity, the ancient campaign pick up against
congregations, against the freedom of association and
the freedom of instruction, anti-Semitism's declama-
tions are hardly less to blame than sectarian hatreds
and the Jacobins' passions. By stumping, every day,
for laws of exception or measures of proscription
against the Jews, anti-Semitism was calling for, in-
sanely, laws of exception against others beside the
Jews. What a people remembers, most easily, of the
laws of exception, is the principle, and this principle
quickly turns against whoever invokes it. Freedom of
instruction or freedom of association, what do French
Catholics lay claim to? They lay claim to common
law. But how can their just claims not be weakened
when, standing beside them and even in the shadow
of the cross, "Catholics" are not afraid of refusing the
benefit of common law to others? In the eyes of non-
Catholics, dissidents, or free thinkers, in the eyes
even of a number of indifferent people, the anti-
Semites' resounding polemics have discredited the
Catholics' most just grievances; for a person is always poorly received who demands for himself the
freedoms that he seems to deny to another.

But if the violent acts of anti-Semitism should

---

[11]Original footnote: See *Israel Among the Nations*, (Calmann
Lévy).

explain the recrudescence of anti-clericalism, will we ever go so far as to say that they justify it? If one presented them as a response to the anti-Semites' provocations, would the laws against Catholic associations or schools be more liberal in our eyes? Who would not feel that this was the worst of sophisms? Is it by intolerance then that one heals intolerance? And when liberals reproach anti-Semites for demanding laws of exception against the Synagogue and the circumcised, how could they pardon men who want to pass analogous laws against the Church and against the Jesuits' pupils? Is it the case that by holding a grudge against Christians, against men or women religious in black or white frocks, intolerance would be less culpable? Or freedom of the equality of rights, which we make it a duty to claim for minority religions, will we deem it equitable to refuse them to the clergy of the majority religion? Who does not see that that would be precisely tantamount to justifying the grievances and accusations of anti-Semites or anti-Protestants, to providing them with dangerous grievances and new weapons against republicans and the Republic itself? Just because anti-Semites want to forbid disciples of rabbis having access to any public office, is that a reason to forbid access to the students of congregations?

To combat laws of exception, we do not want, as far as we ourselves are concerned, to look at those whom they affect. What we deny to the anti-Semites, and also to the socialists, the right to make categories among Frenchmen, to create below a privileged class, a caste of pariahs, – by what contempt of principles could we concede it to anti-clerical hatreds? And what the spirit of freedom would not tolerate on the part of those who call for the integrity of the French race, what would it permit to the Jacobins who wrap themselves in the moral unity of the nation? For anti-Semites or anti-clericals, it is always in the name of national unity that sectarian passions or political factions pretend to cut France into enemy camps, and to remove French rights from their adversaries.

Equality of rights, for all the French, without distinction of religion or origin, class or party, – is the only rule that can guarantee freedom and give France peace. It is hard to have to be reminded of this truth at the dawning of the 20th century. Inasmuch as it might displease the sectarians on the right or left of the political spectrum, it is not at all by measures of proscription or laws of exception, against this or that category of Frenchman, that one is assured of the peace of the country and the unity of the nation. National unity – it is the violence of factions and the intolerance of sects that will put it at peril. National unity, in the present epoch, cannot be sought for in the unity of race or origin, nor in religious uniformity, nor in the monopoly of education. Whatever forms it takes, and whatever sophisms, whatever pretensions it relies on, are merely an outdated archaism or a perilous anachronism in a country like contemporary France. National unity, for modern France, can only be found in religious freedom and equality before the law, in the respect for everyone's rights, in a broad and mutual tolerance that inspires an equal love for the common fatherland in every French person. Instead of an instrument of division or hatred, patriotism must remain a bond of concord and brotherhood, made to bring all the children of France together in a similar sentiment, the filial love of the children of the same mother who all feel equally loved by her and equally at ease with her, who with the same freedoms and same rights can have the same feelings of tenderness and same devotion for her.

To place the patriotism that unites us in opposition to anti-Semitism or anti-Protestantism, to anti-clericalism, to socialism, all which preach hatred, to the excesses of a nationalism even that divides us; to fight, everywhere, against the sectarian mindset and the mindset of intolerance, against the mania of exclusivism and the madness of proscriptions – such, it seems to me, at the present hour, is the primary duty of the French whom prejudices or passion do not blind. Of course, it is not their only duty, but it is the most urgent one; in comparison, all other matters and all other political quarrels seem secondary. To work for religious pacification at the same time as social pacification, to aid in the rapprochement of men as well as the rapprochement of the classes, is still, today, the best, if not the only way, to save freedom and to ensure, by national solidarity, the unity and greatness of France.

Chapter One: The Three "Anti"

Anti-Semitism, Anti-Protestantism, Anti-Clericalism

Resemblance and kinship of anti-Semitism, anti-Protestantism, and anti-clericalism. — I. How one might find analogous passions and reasonings among the three. — How they present themselves, all three of them, under the same aspects and with similar grievances. — II. The religious grievance: intolerance. — The national grievance: denationalization; the tendency to tie the idea of religion to the idea of race. — The political grievance: the accusation of creating a State within the State; religious cosmopolitanism. — The economic or social grievance: "They are too rich; they monopolize wealth and employment." — III. How the grievances of the three "anti" discredit each other. — How, according to them, the principle of our evils would not be within us. — How the three "anti" are engendered and mutually strengthen each other.

Gentlemen,

One of the most saddening things in these sad times of ours is the diffusion among us of what, for lack of better terms, I call the doctrines of hatred: anti-Semitism, anti-Protestantism, anti-clericalism. These hateful doctrines, nourished on all the bile of sectarianism, – patriots and friends of freedom must equally reprove them. Reactionaries or revolutionaries, the fanatics who go around preaching them to the masses, are not only unaware of the rights of freedom, they are in the process of corrupting the French soul, and, if we allow them to, they would denature the genius of France, made of broad tolerance and humane sympathy, in the eyes of other nations.

At the dawn of a new century, which celebrates fraternity and solidarity in so many languages, are there really doctrines of hatred in our country of France? Can it be true that antipathies and enmities between children of the same country have gained such an ascendant that they have turned hatred into a principle?

Alas! it is one of the most disquieting phenomena of our morally-troubled time. Hatred has been glorified, hatred has had its apostles and its panegyrists, in many parties and in opposite camps even.

Religious hatreds, racial hatreds, national hatreds, social hatreds have been hailed around us like the necessary instruments of our emancipation or our regeneration. We have heard, from various sides, – in the name even of forces that seem made to bring men together, in the name of religious faith, in the name of the fatherland, in the name of future society, – we have heard mention of the appeal to "Creative Hatred," to "Fecund Hatred." Paradoxical and immoral combination of words! which is the negation of the laws of nature; for, in the moral order and in the social order, as in the natural order, love alone is fecund, love alone is creative.

I.

This mindset of hatred and violence, almost identical under its different forms, has come to embitter and envenom all our religious, social, or political struggles. With it, the spirit of intolerance has awakened and reappeared among us like revenants of a vanished past, all the old fanaticisms that modern France had thought were forever dead and gone.

It is the same with anti-Semitism in which atavistic prejudices revive and which, more than a century after the Revolution, want to bring us back to a form of medieval intolerance or exclusivism; as if, for lack of religious hatreds, France and Europe were to become a prey to racial hatreds.

It is the same with anti-Protestantism which, in a thriving Republic and in a thriving democracy, was not ashamed to celebrate the politics of the revocation of the Edict of Nantes; as if, any more than the France of the *ancien régime*, modern France was incapable of tolerating denominational dissidences.

It is the same with anti-clericalism which, by its true name, one could call anti-Catholicism or anti-Christianity, which wants to bring us back to the maxims and behaviors of the somber days of the Revolution; as if freedom of thought excluded the freedom to believe and pray, or as if, after having been emancipated from the tutelage of the Church, the State was supposed to subjugate religion and enslave consciences.

Between anti-Semitism and anti-Protestantism on the one hand, and anti-clericalism on the other, the resemblances remain striking, through all the contrasts. They resemble each other like brothers born and nourished by analogous hatreds and passions; they are inimical brothers who, in their very enmity, maintain an attitude of family. All three of them have the same temperament, the same angers, and the same violence; they hardly differ at all, fundamentally, except in the object of their antipathy and passions; because, with the same instincts of intolerance and the same habitudes of exclusivism, they have been to opposite schools and have learnt, by enemy masters, contrary doctrines.

The object of their defiances and of their aversion is different; but their hatreds are made of analogous prejudices and lead them to identical acts of violence.

The parallelism amongst the three "anti" is such that when one makes the effort to analyze them, one is surprised to discover among them the same elements, the same factors, or the same grievances, which it is easy to classify under the same headings or the same rubrics.

What actually are anti-Semitism, anti-Protestantism, anti-clericalism (or anti-Catholicism) composed of? What are their ingredients, their main elements or factors? They are usually three or four in quantity, which we will find in equal measure among each of the "anti," so much so that in order to study them it will be easy for us to apply the same method to all three of them.

Let us try to classify them. They are:

1. Religious or irreligious antipathies, sectarian passions, intolerance of others' beliefs, the desire to use the authority of the law and of public power against those who do not at all think like them;

2. Racial antipathies or national prejudices; a jealous nationalism that accuses diverse denominational groups of denaturing the French spirit, of compromising national unity or the moral unity of the country;

3. Economic rivalries or rancors; existential competition and the struggle for wealth; the desire to evict annoying competition; the reciprocal accusation of holding too large a place in the country and of monopolizing too large a part of the national fortune;

4. Political antipathies and rancors; the passion of power and the ambition of putting one's detested adversaries to the side; the reciprocal accusation of holding a monopoly over public employees and preparing for the enslavement of the country and the State.

Everything that can divide men and embitter them against one another: differences in belief, antipathies of race, the rancors of ancient struggles, national prejudices, social jealousies, political contests, are found to be brought together thus in the three "anti" so as to foment the spirit of suspicion and hatred.

But if sectarian passions, national prejudices, economic rivalries and political battles, if intolerance, prejudices, and hatred form the basis, they do not show themselves in the buff. On the contrary, among the greater part of their adepts, anti-Semitism, anti-Protestantism, anti-clericalism hide behind disinterested motives and noble passions equally. Which explains their vogue among so many simple minds and their ascendant over so many upright souls.

The greatest number of adherents of these three "anti" are but innocent dupes of the prejudices of their world or of their milieu.

Anti-Semitism, anti-Protestantism, anti-clericalism pride themselves, similarly, on serving the cause of truth, justice, and fatherland. The majority do so with an impassioned sincerity, which it is our duty to recognize; but if that is their excuse, that good faith makes them even more redoubtable.

Whether we are listening to their partisans or to their adversaries, the resemblance and kinship of the three "anti" are heard, moreover, by ears that are least prepared for it. Their apostles' homilies, their tribunes' invectives, cause us to hear analogous sufferings, possessing the same anger and the same indignation, almost the same grievances and the same promises.

Anti-Semitism, anti-Protestantism, anti-clericalism, each of the three "anti" are presented to us with the same assurance, like the defender of a religious or philosophical truth, – like the guardian of French tradition and national unity; – like the avenger of public fortune or social mores; – like the champion of State rights and public freedoms. In other words, we find, amongst them, even in their prejudices and their claims, different aspects which I have singled out for you just now: the religious aspect, – the national aspect, – the economic or social aspect, – the political aspect.

The affinity among these three "anti," so seemingly different, is not limited to the similarity of their grievances or prejudices; it extends to their manner of reasoning, to their methods of discussion, to their processes of [engaging in] polemic, because hatreds and passions of the same sort are to be found amongst the three. How to be surprised when one recognizes in them the same bile with the same venom, the same rantings and the same prejudices, the same exclusivism with the same sophistry? They are mixtures made of similar ingredients, similarly made of a bizarre concoction of truths and errors, vile feelings and warped generosities, the entirety of it made bitter and rancid by sectarian hatreds and outdated prejudices.

II.

Before taking them one by one in order to study them successively, it is fitting first to look at what anti-Semitism, anti-Protestantism, and anti-clericalism have in common. The parallel examination of the three "anti" is perhaps the best way in which to understand them and to judge them; and as they are in conflict and as they are ignorant of their kinship, as they detest each other and despise each other reciprocally, nothing can discredit them or disabuse them better then showing them, as if in a mirror, how much they resemble one another. The one revelation of this resemblance would suffice to condemn them and to render them equally odious to us, by making us see that they are equally ugly nearly and equally detestable.

Anti-Semitism, anti-Protestantism, and anti-clericalism, – the first thing that we discover at the bottom of these three "anti," beneath the denominational antipathies and sectarian passions, is, naturally, an equal intolerance of others' beliefs. If none of them have intolerance as a point of departure, each of them leads inevitably to intolerance. This reproach of intolerance, they reject it, all three of them, with an equal rage, and I will be the first to admit it, with an equal sincerity. They defend themselves passionately, with nearly identical distinctions and analogous reasonings, going so far, when needed, the three of them, as to present themselves as the veritable defenders of freedom of conscience against others' intolerance.

Listen to the anti-Semite: he has no problem with the Jewish religion; he has no problem with the Jewish race, with the "Semitic" mindset, with the economic and political preponderance of the Israeli people. For a while, he would assert his respect for the Synagogue and its rabbis.

Listen to the anti-Protestant: he does not wage war on the Reformation and its pastors; he fights only the mindset that invades Protestants, their tendencies toward political hegemony or social preponderance, their efforts to dominate France and to subjugate the State.

Listen to the anti-clerical, he who most often perorates in the cafes: he does not want to destroy the [Catholic] religion, nor the Church; he wants only to resist the traps of the clergy and congregations; he has no other goal than to free the State and secular society from clerical domination. For a while, he will prove to you that by attacking the Catholic convents, schools, and works, he is promoting, in reality, the cause of the Catholic church.

And this nearly identical reasoning of the three "anti," the sheep-like crowd of their adherents repeat it every day with an equal conviction. Intolerance, if one is to believe them, lies in the opposite camp; they do nothing but defend themselves against the fanaticism of their adversaries. They tell themselves, and they persuade themselves all the more easily, that intolerance being common amongst them, it is easier to use the excuse of others' intolerance to hide their own.

The facts show us that despite their desires and their protestations, the three "anti" are, almost equally, driven to intolerance. No matter how much the anti-Semite, anti-Protestant, or anti-clerical defend themselves against the charge, each one of them comes, despite himself, to attack the religion, the worship, the morality of his adversaries. Nor do they spare their dogmas, nor their books; they make no scruple of making use of disloyal weapons, citing the envy of unauthoritative writings, truncated texts, sometimes lying pamphlets. The one incriminates the Talmud or the Cabala, not a page of which he has ever read; he does not blush to repeat inept and perfidious legends about the ceremonies of Judaism, such as ritualistic murder; – the other, proud of a borrowed erudition, claims to rummage through [works of] ancient and modern casuists, extracting, from them, by choice, scabrous passages; or what is more he recurs, triumphantly, to the *Monita Secreta* of the Jesuits, a calumnious work of libel, published by the enemies of the Society of Jesus. The one and the other invoke its history, claiming to point to past acts of intolerance. In both camps, their procedures are identical, and their good faith and intolerance are similar.

One knows that each of the three "anti" treat of the morality of the adverse cult. The anti-Semite lays into Judaic morality, "Talmudic" morality; the anti-Protestant into "Puritanism," into Calvinistic "Pharisaism"; the anti-clerical into Catholic morality, accused by him as being "Jesuitic." To listen to these "anti," one might say that the great religions, having originated from the same biblical trunk, are all three of them nothing but schools of immortality and hypocrisy, made to pervert generations and demoralize peoples.

Added to this religious or anti-religious intolerance is what one is obliged to call, for lack of a better term, a national intolerance, the result of a strict and jealous nationalism. Each of the three "anti" seek to raise, against its adversaries, patriotic defiances and national prejudices, in the name of national unity or the moral unity of the fatherland. Each of the three "anti" contest with its adversaries the title or rights of being French, so much so that to listen to these so-called patriots, the French would end up being a minority in France.

Interrogate the anti-Semite: "The Jew," he will tell you, "is not French. How could he be? He is a Semite, and the French are Aryan; the Jew has nothing in common with us; he is everywhere a foreigner; his fatherland is Jerusalem – or better yet, given he was chased out of Palestine, he is a cosmopolite, someone without a country."

Interrogate the anti-Protestant: "The Protestants," he will tell you, "were expelled or suppressed by Louis XIV; whence do they come those whom we see today? They could not all have come out of their hideouts in Cévennes; they have come to us from Switzerland, Holland, Germany; they are foreigners, imbued with a foreign spirit; their fatherland is Geneva; their heart is with London or Berlin."

Interrogate the anti-clerical: if he dare not assert that all Catholics are foreigners in terms of race or origin for the Catholics are so numerous and they can vaunt having made France, the anti-clerical will apprise you that the clericals, that is, for him, practicing Catholics, are less French citizens than they are subjects of a "foreign sovereign." They are the "ultramontanes"; their heart is with the Vatican; their fatherland is Rome.

And, also, each of the three "anti" accuses his adversaries of falsifying, of denaturing, the French spirit, by altering the French genius, and by imposing on the French a foreign ideal. To believe the anti-Semite, the Jew, that son of Shem, that Oriental, is

in the process of "Judifying" France and French society. To believe the anti-Protestant, the Calvinist and
the Lutheran threaten us with a peril worse than the
mutilation of 1871; they threaten to Germanize the
French soul. To believe the anti-clerical, the Church,
the clergy, the congregations all represent the spirit of
Rome, they strive to extinguish in us every desire of
independence in order to Romanize us, in spite of
ourselves, in order to Latinize us forever. And thus,
according to the three "anti", the French genius, no
matter where it turns, finds itself menaced by denationalization. The Semite Judifies him, the Protestant
Germanizes him, the Catholic Romanizes him.

If the anti-Semite, the anti-Protestant, and the
anti-clerical do not originate from a position of extreme nationalism, they all end up, whether they like
it or not, at a jealous nationalism. Do we need to point
out the similarity of their arguments and the analo-
gousness of this national grievance, which one finds
in this way under nearly identical forms amongst the
three "anti"? All three tend to connect religion to
race, in order consequently to materialize the religious idea and denature it. All three go to great
lengths to make confession, the object of their antipathies, appear suspect to the naïve patriotism of the
demos, while recalling its foreign origins and repre-
senting it as an instrument of denationalization. They
forget that with similar reasonings there would be
nothing left to being French than to reject, in bloc, all
the elements of our civilization, all the religious, liter-
ary, or political heritage of Israel, Greece, and Rome
in order to return to Druidism and to the "*gui l'an*

neuf."[12] And yet the Druids and the Celts themselves were of course not autochthones in Gaul; in order to please these theoreticians of national exclusivism, we would need to return to the barbarousness and fetishism of cavemen.

To this national grievance is joined, for the three "anti," a political grievance. If one is to believe the anti-Semite, the anti-Protestant, the anti-clerical, – the Jews, the Protestants, and the Catholics pose a risk to the State, as well as to the French spirit; for they all compose "a body," and what is worse an inimical body, a "State within the State," which obeys a watchword of the foreigner.

Here again, let's listen to them, and you will be struck by the identity of grievances and the similarity of accusations.

What does the anti-Semite say? The Jews, the "Universal Israelite Alliance," the High Israelite Bank forms a kind of International, with public and secret lodges which, in favor of the principles of the Revolution and of the all-powerful gold, pursue universal domination. They constitute a State within the State, a Semitic State within the French State, an occult State whose politics and interests are in opposition to the interests of the French nation, an enemy State that menaces France and modern peoples with the worst form of servitude. If we want to assure the independence of the State and the salvation of our nationality, it is urgent to protect the State and the nation against the Jewish peril.

---

[12] *[Au] gui l'an neuf*: an exclamation given at New Year.

What does the anti-Protestant say? The Protestants, today, as under the *ancien régime*, form a political party, affiliated with the foreigner, which obeys the inspirations of the Evangelical Alliance and places its sectarian interests above French interests. They also constitute an International, whose intrigues are discovered in all their politics; they too have become a State within the State; they already have a hand in the government, and they audaciously pursue their old design of subjugating France, which the vigilance of our kings did not allow them to execute under the *ancien régime*, under the cover of principles of the Revolution and laws of the Republic. Does one wish to save the independence of the State, [if so] one must put France on guard against the Protestant danger.

What does the anti-clerical say? The Catholic church, Jesuits, and congregations make up an immense International, which has as its goal the conquest of France and contemporary peoples. Its obstinate dream of domination, which formerly the resistances of the ancient monarchy and the ancient parliaments caused to fail and which the Revolution flattered itself to have broken forever, – the Roman Church has not at all renounced it. The supremacy that it was unable to establish or maintain under the *ancien régime,* it pretends to wrest it by indirect methods, under the cover of modern freedoms, thanks to the blindness of liberals and the weakness of republicans. More than ever, the clergy and congregations create a State within the State, a Roman State within the French State, a theocratic State within the democratic State, an ecclesiastical State inspired by the Middle Ages whose ideas, intentions, and ambitions are irreconcilable with the institutions, interests, the existence even, of the secular State. We are resolved to defend the Republic and to save democracy and the sovereignty of the State; we must, first and foremost, arm the State against the clerical peril.

It is in this way that, under the scourge of analogous terrors, every day the three "anti" loudly denounce, in nearly identical terms, the perils that Jewish cosmopolitanism, Protestant cosmopolitanism, and Catholic cosmopolitanism pose the French State and modern France. They do not realize that by taking them literally, their double accusation of forming an International and forming a State within the State falls, inevitably, on all the great religions. For they all have their own constitution, and they all, at least the greatest and the most elevated among them, claim to address all men and all peoples and are, in that respect, cosmopolites or internationals. This sort of religious cosmopolitanism, denounced by the three "anti," is one of the things that makes the strength and the honor of religion, one of the things also that have made of it an incomparable instrument of rapprochement between peoples, and a marvelous agent of high civilization. Anti-Semites, anti-Protestants, and anti-clericals all equally forget that to claim to forbid a religion from crossing over States' borders is to deny them the very principle of religion and to deny with it the foundation of religious freedom. They do not at all see that, under the pretext of maintaining national independence or of ensuring the supremacy of the State, they lead us to the subservience of conscience by making religion a dependency of the State. Their

defiance of every particular society, of every autono-
mous religious association, their repulsion of what
they call a "State within the State," their pretension to
establish everywhere the omnipotence and supremacy
of the State, pushes them towards a tyrannical statism,
at the same time as towards a suspicious nationalism.
When they do not always see where their ideas lead,
the logic of their principle brings the three "anti" to
identify the nation and the State with a doctrine, to re-
store the unity of beliefs, to call for a religion or an ir-
religion of the State.

Under the pretext of defending national unity
or reestablishing the moral unity of the country, they
claim to run all the French people into the same spiri-
tual mold; they finish by the absorption of the individual and of society by the State; when all is said
and done, they stand for the negation of individual
liberties, the suppression of freedom of the family, of
freedom of instruction, of freedom of association, as
well as of freedom of conscience.

The parallelism among anti-Protestantism, anti-Semitism, and anti-clericalism is found in all their
social or economic grievances, albeit to a lesser degree. Listen to them: each of them accuses his adversaries of holding too important a place in the country
or the State, of holding a monopoly of wealth, employees, power. The Jews, the Protestants, says the
one, are too rich; they monopolize the nation's
wealth. The congregations, says the other, have been
prodigiously enriched; mortmain becomes a public
peril. Billions are thrown in each of their face. And

what is, one asks, the origin of these colossal fortunes? For Jewish financiers, for Protestant bankers, it is, according to the anti-Semite, usury, speculation, agiotage, as much to say: theft. We must return to the ancient customs, we must make them cough it up, according to practices from the good old days. And the congregations, cries the anti-clerical when his turn comes around, whence comes their millions? What shall I say? Whence comes that billion that a provident government has just caused to be collected? The scandalous riches of people who have made a vow of poverty, they proceed from the captation of old men and feeble minds, they have for a source the exploitation of the populace's credulity, when it is not the exploitation of charity. It is time to give back to the nation what has been fraudulently taken from the nation.

Those millions and those billions, what do the Jews, the Protestants, and the clerics do with them? The three "anti" will give us the same response. Those billions are employed to corrupt the country, to corrupt the press, to corrupt parliament. The Jew and the Protestant bribe the anti-Catholic press, the radical or socialist newspapers; the congregations subsidize the reactionary press, the nationalist or anti-Semitic newspapers. We must pull the country up out this depravation; we must free it from the demoralizing domination of these corrupters, even if it means resorting to the violence of confiscation; and neither the anti-Semite nor the anti-clerical escape the confiscation. All is permitted against the Jew or against the Jesuit.

One of the principal causes of the diffusion of

these three "anti" is the struggle for public employment. Everyone knows what the importance of func-
tionarism is for us. France, alas! is in the process of
becoming a country of functionaries. Access to public
administration jobs is one of the rights that our contemporaries covet the most; of all those that guarantee
the French people the Rights of Man and the Rights
of the Citizen, it is perhaps what is most dear to them.
Now, the anti-Semite, the anti-Protestant, and the anti-clerical accuse each of their adversaries of wanting
to monopolize all the jobs. Ask the anti-clerical, he
will tell you that, in the army, in order to have some
chance for advancement, one needs to have been
raised by the Jesuits. Ask the anti-Semite or the anti-Protestant, they will tell you that, in order to be admitted into public administrations, or to have a
chance to start one's career there, one must be Jewish,
one must be Protestant, or at least a Freemason. Each
of us is free to judge for himself just how valid these
reciprocal accusations are. The misfortune of France
and the Republic is that the exclusivism of parties
seems to have given them a foundation. One thing is
certain: it is that Catholics believe that they are, for
fifteen or twenty years now, systematically excluded
from all public office and primarily from all high
public office. Nothing has contributed more to making a large number of them anti-Semitic or anti-
Protestant; nothing poses a greater obstacle to religious pacification.

III.

When we examine their religious grievances, their national grievances, their economic grievances, their political grievances, one sees how much they resemble each other and, in some ways, how the anti-Semite's, the anti-Protestant's, and the anti-clerical's complaints and accusations mutually reflect each other and copy each other. This very resemblance, this sort of kinship in their grievances and in their vows puts us, in advance, on guard against their violence and their excesses. We need only lend them an equal ear in order to feel less anxious for the triple threat that they seem to pose. Instead of frightening us, the simultaneous cries of the anti-clerical, the anti-Protestant, the anti-Semite are intended rather to reassure us. Our country of France cannot incur such diverse dangers at the same time.

If they do not cancel each other out entirely, their accusations and their reciprocal grievances discredit one or another amongst them. The real peril, for France and for the public spirit, is perhaps in reality neither the Jewish peril, nor the Protestant peril, nor the clerical peril; it is the appearance and vogue around us of anti-Semitism, anti-Protestantism, anti-clericalism. This is the phenomenon that our patriotism should be alarmed about, because no matter how much they defend themselves against it, all three of them, almost equally, are doctrines of hatred. If they do not derive uniquely from hatred, they end up inevitably at hatred; they preach hatred and division at the same time as they foment a sectarian mindset and fanaticism.

It would be enough, without examining the merit of their grievances, to have the right to con-

demn them, across the board, as immoral and anti-social doctrines.

They are immoral and anti-social doctrines for
another reason as well, because all three of them, anti-Semitism, anti-Protestantism, and anti-clericalism
teach us that the beginning of our evils and our vices
does not reside with us, – a deceiving and pernicious
doctrine if ever there was one. According to them, the
beginning of society's ills would all be exterior; whatever we need to eliminate exists in the Jewish virus,
the Protestant virus, in the clerical virus; what we
need to extirpate would reside in a foreign body only,
in order for us to recover a perfect moral health. A
simple surgical operation would suffice. Now, such a
doctrine is a sophism that is opposed to every serious
moral reform. France and contemporary society have,
assuredly, need of a moral reform, if not a social reform, but this reform, in order for it to be profound
and efficacious, must bear on ourselves, on our ideas,
on our mores and on our habits, on our private life
and on our pubic life. Otherwise, all political reforms
and all constitutional revisions, all legal reforms as
well as all revolutions, will remain sterile.

Instead of recognizing the truth, each of the
three "anti" show us a scapegoat on which they are
pleased to pile all our sins and to make responsible
for all our ills. It is a borrowing from Semitic traditions of something that is difficult to praise them for.
There is today in France, for the masses and, alas!
sometimes also for the elite, two scapegoats that, in
opposite camps, are made responsible for all the problems that traverse the country. These two scapegoats,

do we need to name them? It is the Jew, and it is the Jesuit. To believe the anti-Semite and the anti-clerical, who equally enlarge and magnify the object of their hatred, they would be the two great powers of our times. Nothing in public life would happen, apparently, without their instigation, or without their authorization. They would hold the invisible strings of all intrigues; one would sense their evil hand in all contemporary agitations. The politicians we see, the renowned journalists, the ministers, the party chiefs would be merely docile instruments or the inert marionettes in the hands of those occult puppet masters who fight for control and supremacy amongst themselves. The Jew and the Jesuit, double object of superstitious terrors, are thus two scarecrows, like two specters, not to mention bogey men, whom our sectarian passions and our ignorant credulity cause us to spot everywhere in the shadows.

The anti-Semite and the anti-clerical make, in this way, an analogous conception, equally narrow and equally false, of politicians and contemporary history. Dupes of Judaic terror or victims of Jesuit terror, they do not understand the facts that they are witness to; they grasp neither the proportions nor the scope; they distort the meaning and the importance. For the events that pass before their prejudiced eyes, the anti-Semite and anti-clerical provide an infantile explanation to the masses. In an era when the rivalries between peoples and the exploitation of vast continents, when scientific inventions and competition between classes are in the process of changing the face of the world, among all the forces that stir on the expanded scene of history, they distinguish merely two that their fright disproportionately exaggerates, and to which their myopia and their mania attribute all the instigations and all the movements of politics, all the revolutions and all the ills of modern society.

All the while fighting amongst themselves, they find common ground thereby to pervert public opinion, to distract it from enormous and urgent problems, and necessary and efficacious reforms, in favor of superannuated quarrels and petty and sterile disagreements. With both eyes fixed on the past, they make equal appeal to prejudices and ignorance, to rancor and fanaticism, everything that divides and disunites.

If only for this reason, I would be justified in asserting that they are anti-patriotic and anti-national doctrines, as well as immoral and anti-social doctrines. For they do not stop at denaturing the meaning of the facts and falsifying public opinion; under the pretext of delivering us and saving us, they preach to us both discord and violence. Anti-Semitism, anti-Protestantism, anti-clericalism are in agreement in seeing salvation only in the extinguishment of their adversaries.

Each of the three "anti" repeat in the same way:

This house is mine, and you must leave.

To listen to them, the house, in other words-France, is too small to lodge all its children at the same time. Each of the "anti" aspire to expel its adversaries; each asks for laws of proscription and confiscation against them and, as intolerance begets intolerance and hatred provokes hatred, anti-Semitism, anti-Protestantism, and anti-clericalism mutually engender and nourish each other. They are in a certain way the product of one another. The respond to each other like an echo. Each of them excuses its hatred and violence by others' violence and hatred. Ask the anti-Semite or the anti-Protestant how they justify their sectarian passions; they will tell you that it is by the heinous predications and calls for intolerance by anti-clericalism. Ask the anti-clerical whence comes its indignations and its angers against Catholics and the clergy; it will respond, most often, that they come from the fits of rage and furies of anti-Semitism. One could maintain that the principal factor of anti-clericalism is, at the present hour, anti-Semitism, just as the primary factor of anti-Semitism is, today, anti-clericalism. We have seen it quite clearly these last years. The recrudescence of anti-clericalism – I hope to demonstrate it – came out of the violence of the anti-Semitic campaign, following the Dreyfus Affair.

I will also dare to say that the best way to combat anti-Semitism or anti-Protestantism is to repel anti-clericalism. And similarly, the surest way to fight anti-clericalism is to reprove anti-Semitism and anti-Protestantism. Whoever claims to wage battle against one of these three "anti" must declare war on all three equally.

Do we want to make France peaceful again and free ourselves from these doctrines of hatred, we must know how to raise ourselves above prejudices and sectarian passions, by claiming, boldly and loyally, the same freedom and the same rights for all

French people, without distinction of origin, class, or religion.

Chapter 2. Anti-Semitism

Principal aspects of anti-Semitism. — I. Religious grievance. — The Jew has two morals. — Anti-Semitism and Christian chari- ty. — The Jews and the secularization of contemporary soci- eties. — The Jews and Freemasons. — II. The Jewish mindset. — What does one understand by that, and what are the types? — The Jewish mindset is a stranger to Judaism? — How is it that often this has nothing strictly Jewish about it? — III. The national and political grievance. — The Jew is a foreigner. — Semites and Aryans. — Jewish particularism and the spirit of the tribe. — Jewish solidarity and cosmopolitanism. — IV. The social and economic grievance. — The Jew is a parasite. — The High Bank and financial monopoly. — The Jewish proletariat. — The Jews and competition. — How anti-Semitism led to a forgery of socialism. — V. Conclusion. — What solutions does anti-Semitism offer us? — There is but one solution, freedom and equality. — What would be different if there were no Jews in France? — On the so-called Judaization of contemporary so- cieties.

Gentlemen,

Anti-Semitism is the type of what I call a doc- trine of hatred; for this reason, it is natural that we be- gin with it. It is a vast subject, very complex, and one that is difficult to cover in one hour. I have already, for my own part, discoursed on it and written about it multiple times;[13] I will probably be obliged to repeat myself, on more than one point. Today I plan to focus on France, and I will even, when speaking only about France, be condemned for being brief, perhaps super-

---

[13]Original footnote: See *Israel Among Nations* (Calmann Lévy) and *Anti-Semitism*, a conference given at the Catholic Institute (same publisher).

ficial; I will keep myself to a cursory review, so to speak, touching only on the most salients aspects of the topic.

Anti-Semitism presents itself to us under three or four principal aspects: it offers itself, first of all, as the avenger of Christianity and religion; it offers itself, as well, as the champion of the fatherland and national unity; it offers itself, finally, as the defender of the public weal and social mores. We will examine, successively, each of these aspects, so as to judge on what these pretensions of anti-Semitism are based.

I.

Let us take the religious aspect, or rather the religious grievance, of anti-Semitism first. Anti-Semites do not like it when one repeats that their campaign has as a point of departure a religious sentiment, to say nothing of a religious prejudice.

It would be unjust, of course, to pretend, as many people do, that anti-Semitism is, uniquely, a reminiscence of old prejudices from the Middle Ages. But, from another point of view, it is incontestable that, in spite of everything, religious antipathies occupy a place, and sometimes even a very large one.

Each "anti," as I have already noted, is soon made to attack the religion that it finds before it. It is in this way that the anti-Semites hold a grudge against Judaism, its cult, its traditions, its books, its morality.

Let's take its morality: there is a reproach that

is made, every day, against the Jews, their rabbis, their teachings, the Talmud, sometimes even the Bible. They say: the Jew has two moralities; it has a morality for its people, and it has a morality for others, a morality for the *goyim*. You will notice, in passing, that anti-Semites have a singular preference for Hebraic terms; that gives to their grievances a kind of local color which creates an illusion; it makes believe that they are versed in the reading of biblical texts, and Talmudic ones necessarily; but this anti-Semitic erudition is completely superficial; it is verbal only; it is for the most part merely an illusion.

So the Jew has two moralities: one for its own people, one for others. The Bible clearly teaches that one must love one's neighbor; it is a precept that pre-dates Christianity, and, as with many others, it is a point which the Gospel continues from the Old Testament. But how must one understand "one's neighbor"? According to the anti-Semites, it is quite simple: the neighbor for a Jew is a Jew; for him, to love his neighbor is to love a Jew. – And they will cite other texts to you that are more or less authentic. It is yet another one of those things to point out in all those campaigns of the "antis," the abuse of more or less authentic, more or less truncated texts. I do not have the time here to delve into the merit of such a grievance. It will suffice to say that Jewish mortality and the books that are authoritative in Judaism, the Bible to begin with, teach, categorically, the love of one's neighbor, understood in a broad sense. The Bible speaks even of the love for a stranger who lives among the Jews. The fundamental notion of Judaism when it comes to morality is the idea of justice and,

by itself, that idea of justice extends to all social relations.

Without pausing for too long on this question,
we will turn it around on the anti-Semites; we will ask
them, those who accuse Judaism of having two
moralities, whether the anti-Semites do not have but
one and the same morality vis-à-vis Jews and vis-à-
vis Christians.

What is the virtue that is, to a certain extent,
the essence of Christianity? It is charity; – Christian
charity, these two words are for us so intimately united that it is almost impossible for us to separate them.
Now, this Christian charity, does the anti-Semite believe that he is obliged to extend it to the Jews even?
Let's read its newspapers, is opuscules, its books: you
will see how the anti-Semite understands brotherhood
vis-à-vis the Jews. Also, I will allow myself, in my
quality as a Christian, – for I am honored to call myself a Christian, – to state that anti-Semitism, inasmuch as a doctrine, has no right to make references to
Christianity and the Gospel, understanding that by doing so it would harm Christianity or the Gospel to
conceive of them as lacking in charity. "Though I
speak with the tongues of men and of angels," said
the Apostle, "and have not charity, I am become as
sounding brass, or a tinkling cymbal."[14] A brass instrument that sounds the chase and the quarry, empty
and harsh cymbals that provoke hatred and violence,
for lack of charity, – these are the loudest voices of
our anti-Semites, am I not right?

---

[14]Though I speak... 1 Corinthians 13:1, KJV.

Religious grievance, I willingly admit it, often takes, in contemporary anti-Semitism, a more serious shape. The Jews, one says, are the born enemies of Christianity and Christian civilization. As such, they are, everywhere, in the first row of adversaries of the Church and institutions animated by the Christian spirit. They are the promoters or lessors of cultivated land, the intellectual or material purveyors of sects and parties who, under the appearance of secularization of the State and confessional neutrality, work to ruin the religious spirit together with the Christian faith and traditions. The Jews, in a word, are the great agents, not to mention the great entrepreneurs, of the "de-Christianization" of contemporary peoples.

The Jew, as the anti-Semite usually adds, is the master and inspirator of an invading society that, at least in Latin countries, incarnates a hatred of religion and Christianity, it incarnates Freemasonry in other words. Jews and Freemasons, for a number of our anti-Semites, are one and the same. The assimilation has become banal and, in order to affirm it in everyone's eyes, we have recently seen rise up in Paris, on a par with the "Grand Orient," the "Grand Occident," haughty citadel of anti-Semitism.

It is a serious grievance that neither the Christian, who has a legitimate desire to preserve the Christian faith, nor the politics that believe that a people cannot forgo any religious experience without impunity, are insensitive to. Among all the grievances stirred up by anti-Semitism today, it is one of those that the Jews would have the greatest interest in seeing cast aside, as well as one of those that merits their greatest antipathy or their greatest defiance, among the least hateful of people even. Those Jews who do not understand it at all, those who, in order to push back against the anti-Semites' aggressions, are made the propagators of anti-clericalism, have gone down the wrong road; they provide nourishment and arguments to the anti-Semites; for, as I will need to repeat more than once, anti-clericalism and anti-Semitism have the principal effect of provoking and reinforcing one another.

But this grievance, is it as well-founded as a number of our contemporaries believe? Are the Jews really everywhere the promoters of the secularization or the de-Christianization of modern peoples? Is that not in fact something that goes back to the 18th century and the French Revolution, in other words to an era when the Jews had no influence among us, when the most ardent anti-Semite would not dare speak of a Jewish preponderance? Was the 18th century or the French Revolution ever actually imbued with the Jewish spirit? And as some people are fine with identifying Israel's actions with that of Freemasonry, is this assimilation between the Universal Israelite Alliance and the Grand Orient, between the Jewish spirit and the Masonic spirit, really justified? It is a matter on which I will not insist here because I have treated of it elsewhere, in a discourse given at the Catholic Institute of Paris.[15] Whatever opinion one might hold of Freemasonry, its purpose, its ascendant; whether

---

[15]Original footnote: See *Anti-Semitism*, a discourse given at the Catholic Institute (Calmann Lévy), p. 9-21. Cf. *Israel Among Nations*, chap. 3.

one considers it as one of the powers of the day, or whether one regards the influence that some people attribute to it as largely overrated, one thing is incontrovertible: that despite its ceremonial legend and Hebrew names or titles, which its adepts love to cover themselves in, Freemasonry has nothing Jewish about it, neither in its origins, nor in its organization, nor in its inspiration. Originated in England, at the beginning of the 18th century, and at first billeted in aristocratic beds, continental Freemasonry, despite its sumptuous maxims of universal brotherhood, has for a long time now remained closed to the Jews. Today even, in Germany, and Romania above all, a number of lodges still turn Israelites away, so much so that Romanian Jews who want to don the Masonic apron are forced to found Jewish lodges exclusively for themselves.

The anti-Semites' obstinacy in identifying Freemasons and Jews, in what they call Judeo-Freemasonry, only shows their lack of good faith or ignorance. If history and the facts prevent considering Freemasonry as a Jewish institution, founded or directed by the Jews, in the Jews' interest, anti-Semitism falls back on the lineage of the Jewish spirit and the Masonic spirit. To hear them speak, the lodges, on the continent at least, in Latin countries predominately, would be merely docile instruments in the hands of Israel anymore. When, breaking with Freemasonic traditions, the Grand Orient rejected the authority of the Grand Architect of the Universe, the French lodges would have obeyed the suggestions of the Jewish spirit, just as if the Synagogue had abjured ancient monotheism and just as if the Jew, in revolt against his ancestors' God, would have had one aspiration anymore – that of dethroning Jehovah.

The Jewish spirit is, in effect, the object of fears and repulsion, not only by anti-Semites, but by a large number of our contemporaries. What I refer to as the Jewish spirit, one could repeat it, *mutatis mutandis*, as the "Protestant spirit" and the "clerical spirit." Religious or political, the polemics engaged in by the three "anti" spill a lot of ink on what they call the "Jewish Spirit," – the "Protestant Spirit" – the "clerical Spirit." That in itself should give us pause.

II.

Is there a Jewish spirit? If there is, in what does it consist? What are its traits, and what are the signs of it? – A singular thing, when one wants to analyze what one means, for the most part, by the Jewish spirit, we find that on a number of points the Jewish spirit incriminated by the anti-Semites is the negation of the doctrines and traditions of Judaism.

What, in effect, is the "Jewish spirit" in the eyes of a great number of our fellow citizens? It is, and we will come back to this in a moment, a foreign spirit, hostile to the genius of our race. It is, at the same time and by the same token, a spirit of revolt and a spirit of negation; – certain people, we will soon see them, have the same opinion of the Protestant spirit. By consequence, the Jewish spirit, – and for analogous reasons, the Protestant spirit, – would be nothing but a dissolvant for our France and for Christian Europe: to give it a free field, to permit it to

"Judaize" our laws and our institutions, is not only to compromise national power, it is to ruin the bases of French society.

If the Jewish spirit were truly a spirit of revolt and negation, if the Jews were encountered everywhere at the highest ranks of destroyers and levelers, or if they slyly pushed enemies of the current political and social order into the shadows, it could be explained by the historical education that Christian peoples have, themselves, given to Israel, by the sufferings that the political or social order has for the longest time inflicted on them, and by the resentments that it has left them with. How would the Jews not feel defiance or rancor for the institutions or authorities that have kept them, for so long and so obstinately, outside the common law, not to mention outside humanity? It is enough to think on the last twelve or fifteen centuries of persecution and abasement, and one will understand what the massacres and butcheries of the past could have left on the Jew, on his intelligence, on his soul, on his ideas, – a mark, and, if one wishes, stigmas, which the brief years of emancipation have not yet had enough time to efface. The trace of so many centuries of suffering and humiliation cannot disappear, all of a sudden, by the promulgation of a decree, or by the vote of a law of franchisement.

How to be surprised by the "ferment of revolt that boils" in so many Israelite hearts still, when one recalls how long and hard the period of abasement and oppression has been for Israel; how recent and sometimes incomplete, how precarious and disputed it is still, for a number of Jews, their tardy emancipa-

tion? After all, they are, for the most part, the enfranchised, or the children of the enfranchised; they often
resent the slavery of their fathers, and, so as to be
more sure that they do not lose their freedom, they
keep up their guard against parties or powers that
have for the longest time kept them in irons, and who,
sometimes still, seem as though they want to put them
in chains again. How to be scandalized that the Revolution and the spirit of the Revolution holds sway
over the majority of Western Jews, sometimes even
on the "great Jews" whose fortune and interests are
openly threatened by revolutionary demands? That in
our political battles or our social contests many Jews
seem inclined towards parties or doctrines whose
temerity is designed precisely to frighten us? Is that
really a racial trait? And can one see in it the mark of
the Jewish spirit or the Semitic genius? If the tradition
of old prophets is not foreign to it, if the "son of
Zion" has bequeathed to the dispersed tribes, with
messianic hopes, a vague ideal of social justice, the
revolutionary or social tendencies of a number of contemporary Jews derive from a less ancient source;
they come, primarily, from a quite simple fact, which
is that the Jews owe their enfranchisement to the
French Revolution, and that the men who threaten to
put back on them the outdated yoke of laws of exception are, habitually, the declared adversaries of the
Revolution and of what is called, rightly or wrongly,
the modern spirit.

If it is in this that the Jewish spirit consists,
one would be unable to recognize in it an ethnic character, a racial trait. But it is just the opposite: in the
countries of the Middle East where they live isolated,

closed in their old Jewish quarters, under the authority of their law and their rabbis, as I have more than once remarked, the Jews have remained rather conservative, defiant of novelties, respectful of tradition, sometimes even slaves to routine. To accuse them of or glorify them for being instigators of the French Revolution, pioneers of new ideas, is to misunderstand them. Sephardim or Ashkenazim, it was the same, formerly, for Western Jews, the contemporaries of Spinoza or Moïse Mendelssohn. Far from having set the new world in motion, the Jewish spirit felt the effect of said impulsion. As for Revolution, the Jew of modern times is not so much the initiator as the imitator. As I have written recently,[16] in the 18th century the Jews were so tightly bound and tied by the Talmud and ritual observations that, if we had not cut their ties, or if we had not handed them the scissors and files in order to sever them themselves, they would never perhaps have had the strength to sever them. Let's not reverse roles here; it's not the Jew who has freed Christian thought and turned contemporary societies upside down, it is Christian thought, or rather, modern thought, that has freed the Jew.

The spirit of innovation has reached him, almost everywhere, from without; but once he was touched by it, one need not be surprised that he has often followed the adversaries of religious or monarchic traditions. How could it be that the Christian idea would recruit its defenders from among the Jews, or that the *ancien régime* and ancient monarchy would have partisans among them? And how could religious or political escapees of the ghetto not defy the tradi-

---

[16]Original footnote: See *Israel Among Nations*.

tions of a past that left them such cruel memories? That defiance toward ideas or institutions of the past, will we not find it as well, for similar reasons, among other victims of the *ancien régime,* among our French Protestants, so much so that our anti-Semites are not afraid to assimilate the Huguenot mindset to that of the Jew?

That the vexations or sufferings felt under the *ancien régime* have predisposed the Jews to rise up against or defy the institutions of the past, does it follow that the principal trait of the Jewish spirit is to wage battle against the Christian spirit and the religious spirit, pushed to an extreme of militant materialism? Can one assert, with a talented writer,[17] that if the Hebrew of Biblical antiquity "was the deist (or better yet, the theist) type," the Jew is today the "irreconcilable Enemy of God?"

Who are the men most often presented to us as the legitimate and authentic representatives of the Jewish spirit? They are Spinoza, Heine, Lassalle, Karl Marx, to cite only the dead, that is, writers usually or agitators detached from Judaism and the Jewish tradition. What would the Jews of Amsterdam who struck Spinoza with "Herem" have said, if one had said to them that a day would come when this disciple of *goyim,* excommunicated by the Synagogue, would be presented as an honored representative of the Jewish spirit? What is true of Spinoza is even more true of Heine or Marx. These are Jews detached from the Jewish tradition, those whom I have termed, in *Israel*

---

[17]Original footnote: Maurice Muret, *The Jewish Spirit,* Paris, Perrin, 1901.

Among Nations, the "de-Judaized" Jews, that is, men who in contact with us and under the influence of our Western civilization have abandoned the beliefs and traditions of their fathers in order to replace them with novel ideas and notions, borrowed from a setting unfamiliar to Judaism.

These de-Judaized Jews, formed in our schools, – it is permissible to discover in them the persistent mark of Israelite origins and even to detect in them traces of Jewish or Hebrew genius. The error, if not the paradox, however, is to regard them as the only or the principal representatives of the Jewish spirit. As faithful or as skillfully depicted as they can be, the portraits of all these Jewish deserters of Judaism, they would not represent to us the modern Jew, but a false image, because incomplete, showing us only one side, and precisely the least Jewish side. Now, this error is the error of the majority of our writers and our polemicists. When they want to depict the character or the spirit of the modern Jew, they put at a distance, unconsciously or on purpose, all the Jews who have remained faithful to the God of the Bible, as if it was necessary in order to personify the Jewish spirit to address themselves, uniquely, to baptized Jews or to renegades of the Jewish faith. It is a little as if, in order to study the Catholic spirit, one chose Voltaire, Diderot, and the Encyclopedists who graduated from Jesuit colleges to represent Catholics. I know that the anti-Semites have in mind the race and not the religion of the Jews; but, with the Jews, race and religion are difficult to separate entirely inasmuch as they are, in a certain way, the product of each other. It is their religion that has formed and preserved the Jews; and when one sees in their religion the expression only of the genius of their race, it is hardly in conformance with history or reason not to recognize in it one of the factors of the Jewish spirit.

To make of the Jew, as the anti-Semites do, the negating spirit *par excellence* and the "irreconcilable enemy of God," one must by a sort of historical and philosophical paradox isolate the Jew from the Synagogue, cut him off from his Bible, from his Talmud, and from all the literature properly called Jewish.

Assuredly, the spirit of negation or of skepticism is frequent among Western Jews who, in contact with us or with our schools [of thought], have emptied themselves, so to speak, of all the beliefs of their ancestors and all the traditions of Israel, without anything having filled that emptiness yet. It is for that reason undoubtedly that some of our contemporaries feel authorized to write that the contemporary Jew is an "ardent demolition contractor." If that is true of more than one Western Jew, these negative penchants or these destructive instincts do not originate with their race; they have nothing, in themselves, of the Semitic or the Judaic in them; they originate predominately from history, from ancient hatreds or lively rancors accumulated among the children of Israel by the long persecution of the Middle Ages and by the long-lasting abasements of the *ancien régime*. It is difficult to recognize in it a Jewish philosophy or politics. Religious or political, these negative doctrines, – for those same revolutionary Israelites who can boast of possessing a doctrine, – have not emerged spontaneously from the bosom of Israel; they have, almost always, come to it from without. I can cite a recent and striking example. One has often reproached the Russian Jews during the last twenty years of the 19th century of being inclined to "nihilism" and to anarchism. Jewish emigrants, pushed by intolerance or by poverty from the shores of the Baltic Sea or the Black Sea to the New World, have been accused, more than once, of having brought this sort of theoretical nihilism with them, from autocratic Russia into free America. Now, this anarchic nihilism, alien to their coreligionists of the West or the Middle East, where did these Russian Jews find it? Was it in their synagogues, in their *heder* or in their Talmud-Torah? No, it was in Russian schools, in imperial universities, among Bakunine and Kropotkine compatriots.[18]

Some of them exist among the Western Jews, the Jews of France or Germany, as well as those of Russia. If they often let themselves be led to revolutionary theories and negative ideas, if they sometimes become their champions or apostles, the Jews are rarely their inventors. At most, they sometimes give them, like Karl Marx, a shape, a new mode. Whoever makes the effort to examine the Jews, country by country, State by State, discovers that Jewish radicalism maintains, habitually, a local color, according to the land it comes from. It would be opportune for anti-Semites to stick to their preferred thesis, to say that the Jews invent nothing, that they live only by borrowing, that as far as ideas and as far as industry is concerned, the Semite is never anything more than a

---

[18]Original footnote: See *Empire of the Tsars and the Russians*, tome II, book VI, chapter 1.

courtier. Something that in other domains is nothing but an inept and iniquitous accusation would ordinarily be justified in politics and in revolution.

The Jewish spirit, if one understands by this the spirit of negation and destruction, has nothing for the most part of the truly Jewish in it. If there are materialist Israelites, atheistic Israelites, these sons of Israel, traitors to the ancient faith of Judah, are far from having imported materialism or atheism among us; they breathed it, habitually, in our atmosphere; they picked it up from their non-Jewish neighbors, the Christians, the "Aryans," so that, to trace it back to its origins and follow it to the source, this Jewish spirit derives from the "Aryan" spirit. Most often this so-called Jewish spirit is quite simply the spirit of the 18th century and of the Revolution. If, to this spirit of the Revolution that for many of our contemporaries is still identified with the modern spirit, something particularly Jewish or Hebraic is to be blended from among the Israelites, it is, over and above a natural aversion for the *ancien régime*, – a comment that has often been made – the faith in Progress, the great modern dogma, to which the Jew was prepared for a long time now by the visions of its prophets and by its messianic aspirations. In order to become ardent proselytes of this human faith in Progress, it sufficed the sons of Israel to read the Bible in the light of the Encyclopedists and philosophers. They thought they had found, in the promises of the gentiles' profane seers, the predictions of the "nabis" of the Jordan [river]. In this way is explained how a modern man so easily emerges from the little Jewish routine of the old Jewries, – in certain respects, the most modern of moderns. Nevertheless, in matters of negation or political or philosophical radicalism, the Jew has been our pupil, and not our master. It is not us, in spite of what the anti-Semites think, who become Judaized by our contact with him; it is rather he who becomes "de-Judaized" by his contact with us. If there is, really, between us and him, contagion of skepticism and materialism, there would be injustice, on our part, in holding him responsible; for the germs of this moral evil, – they contracted them from us, they did not give them to us.

But is it true that all modern Jews are zealots of negative doctrines, enemies of the idea of God, and staunch champions of the great revolt against all authority?[19]

If a number of modern Jews are adepts of materialism, it is hardly true to say the same thing of the Western Jews, more or less "de-Judaized" in our schools. Nothing seems to have changed since antiquity. The Jews who have remained faithful to the Talmud have an ancient name to designate them from their brothers who have become materialists; they call them the *Apikorim*, that is, the Epicureans, indicating by this sobriquet the foreign origin of materialism in Israel. As for myself, I have visited in Europe, Asia, Africa, the majority of large Jewries from the Middle East; I can state that the Atheistic Jew, the Jew who is

---

[19]Original footnote: In order to know the Jewish spirit as it truly is, one would need to be in contact with Jewish milieus and be familiar with Jewish literature through the Israelite newspapers, with their "jargon" or neo-Hebrew language. Now, according to what is translated in Israelite reviews or journals, all this Jewish literature remains devoted to the idea of One God.

an "irreconcilable enemy of God," is very rare to
come by. And, even in the West, have all Jews really
turned to atheism in religion, to collectivism or anarchy in politics? Is it the same for those in England, for
example, which for twenty years has served as a place
of refuge for so many thousands of fugitive Israelites?
Disraeli, that little Sephardic Jew, dressed as an English lord, who is taken sometimes as one of the representatives of the Jewish spirit, was neither an atheist
nor a socialist in spite of democratic tendencies; and
the English Jews who remained faithful to Judaism
are no more so than he. Many, like Beaconsfield, support the conservative party. In the United States,
where their numbers will continue to grow, Jews, like
Christians, are divided between the two great political
parties. The fact is that (all Jewish history suggests it)
the Jew varies according to the country, as according
to the times. Of the three principal factors of a civilization or of a literature, according to Taine, – race,
environment, the time, – the two last are, when all is
said and done, those that have the most influence over
the modern Jew. Here, as in all things, the anti-
Semites' error is to apply to the sons of Israel their iniquitous and coarse theory in bloc. Jews or Christians,
Protestants or Catholics, their thinking and contemporary activity are more complex than the anti-Semites,
anti-Protestants, or anti-clericals imagine.

Who among us can be surprised, as regards
the Jews, when the suppleness, the flexibility, the gift
of adaptation are qualities that their adversaries contest the least in the Israelites. Like the modern spirit
itself, which in many respects is only a reflection of
it, the Jewish spirit uneasily lets itself be contained by

cut and dry formulas. It is all the truer given that the Jews are found in all the philosophical or social schools of the 19th century, the century when they had to fight the most for their emancipation. Israel hasn't really ever acted in bloc except against adversaries of its enfranchisement, and still, despite its legendary solidarity, the enemies of the Jews have often found accomplices even in the ranks of the Jews.

Is it necessary to show, by examples, that the Jewish spirit is not ineluctably atheistic or materialistic? Without resorting to Spinoza, that great religious soul in his fashion, whom the anti-Semites love to cite the name of without perhaps understanding his doctrines, we find Moses Mendelssohn, less great certainly than the philosopher of the Hague, but nearer to us and representative of the Jewish spirit in quite another way. The promoter of the reformation of Judaism, he whom one called the Socrates of Berlin, Mendelssohn, a friend of Lessing and, as one knows, the prototype of his "Nathan der Weise," was the author of *Phaedon* and the eloquent defender of the idea of God and the immortality of the soul. How many Christians would have dared, in the 18th century, to rewrite *Phaedon* in this way? If Mendelssohn had had the courage to do so, it was because he was still imbued with the veritable Jewish spirit; and if skepticism or materialism have prevailed, since then, among so many of his similars, it is because they were detached from the tradition of Israel; it is because, despite the prohibition of old German rabbis, they opened the profane books and tasted the forbidden fruits of modern science. Just like the Jews of Russia, I have had plenty of occasions to note it, it is effectively at the University, at the *Alma Mater*, founded by the Church or by the State, that the Jews of Germany or Austria picked up their radical leanings towards nihilism.

Would the ancient faith in Jehovah really have deserted the Synagogue? Or is it no longer but an isolated case of intellectual atavism among the emancipated Jews of the Occident? Is every civilized Jew an enemy of God at the same time as a contemnor of the idea of the fatherland?[20] Focusing only on France, I could cite the name of a man of virtue, a poet that we accompanied to the cemetery of Montmartre just several weeks ago, who was, for nearly half a century, the friend of J. Simon and Pasteur: M. Eugène Manuel. He was not ashamed of his Israelite origins, and, all the while remaining conversant in whatever makes the honor of modern civilization, he never denied the God of the prophets. He had been, in his youth, with five other young men, all French like him, one of the founders of the Universal Israelite Alliance, which the hateful ignorance of anti-Semites would construct into a bogeyman, and whose schools in Asia and America render so many services to European culture and the French language. The author of *Ouvriers* has never sung anything but noble things: God, soul, family, fatherland, chaste love, social

---

[20]Original footnote: I would be reproached for not mentioning here the name of a French Israelite, Joseph Salvador, in whom were so curiously combined the ancient hopes of Israel and the highest modern aspirations. No son of Judah, perhaps, would have had more right to be admitted as a representative of the Jewish spirit in the 19th century than the author of *Rome, Paris, Jerusalem*, the original thinker who dreamt of a sort of synthesis of the Bible, the Gospel, and contemporary science.

peace; that is to say, practically, everything that one assures us is the negation of the Jewish spirit.

Eugène Manuel was a poet, and poets, a race of artists and dreamers, are repugnant to the idea of banishing God and the soul from their dreams. Does one want a philosopher? It would be easy to cite one while still focusing on France. I will name one that I knew as well, a modest man and a sage, like Manuel, and like him, a Frenchman and a patriot, who knew how to associate whatever there was of the most elevated traditions of Israel with a high modern culture: M. Adolphe Franck. Whenever God or the soul seemed to be in question, at the Academy of Moral Sciences, this old philosopher, who had learnt how to read from the Talmud, defended them with an accent of faith and indignation that surprised his listeners, not to mention made an indelible mark on them, in those cold academic sessions. One might have imagined oneself listening to a prophet on the banks of the Jordan. I have never known a more ardent champion of the idea of God. We have, in France, a national League Against Atheism that M. Arthur Desjardins presided over, before he was taken from us. Does anyone know who founded this league against atheism? It was founded by a Jew, M. Adolphe Franck, with the support of J. Simon and the participation of many scholars of divers persuasions, M. Ch. Wadington among others, he too a spiritualist philosopher whose example demonstrates that the Protestant spirit is not always negative, nor always sectarian, anymore than the Jewish spirit is. A number of others among the members of the League Against Atheism are Jews and Protestants from Paris and its outlying areas which, in order to fight against the coarse materialism of the masses, are not afraid to lend a helping hand to the Catholics. And something that people will allow me to call out, one of the last published documents by this League Against Atheism for its adherents is a study, translated from Italian, entitled *Science and Faith*; and as it happens, these pages wherein the faith in God is glorified with an eloquent enthusiasm are from the quill of an Israelite, M. Luigi Luzzatti, the scholarly Italian economist who succeeded Gladstone, an associate of the Institute of France. Such examples suffice to demonstrate that in similar matter, if one does not wish to exceed the limits of truth and justice, one must be careful not to make hasty generalizations instead of rushing to line up all the Jews or all the Protestants in bloc behind the banners of atheism and cosmopolitanism.

To the man curious to grasp the Jewish spirit, or the tendencies and aspirations of the contemporary Jew, in philosophy, in politics, in social science (as much at least as the Jews differ from their compatriots of different origin), I would willingly advise bringing one's attention to the Jews of Italy, England, and the United States. And for this reason that they are countries where the Jew is not bothered by the violences of anti-Semitism, where, no longer having to fear the revenants of the past, the oppressed of so many centuries can let down their guard to a certain degree; whereas in countries where the battle between ancient traditions and modern institutions is still ardent, where religious freedom and civil equality does not yet seem above all assault, the enfranchised of the ghetto, anxious for recently acquired rights, and irritated by their adversaries' insults or disdain, are inclined to battle against everything they believe to be hostile to Israel; and as they arrive dressed for war, they pass, they too, without scruple, from the defensive to the offensive. What one depicts for us as the Jewish spirit is often nothing more than the combative humor of men who, feeling or believing themselves in peril, find themselves obliged, vis-à-vis their old oppressors, to remain on a war footing.

It may be that, among us, in France, the Jew, like the Protestant, has not always known how to free himself from the rancors of the past and the apprehensions of the future. For a Jewish spirit or a Protestant spirit, the passions, antipathies, resentments, and sectarian exclusivism that are attributed to them are, for the most part, the result of this confessional state of war in which we live in France, alas! since the time of the crusades preached by the anti-Semites.

Anti-Semites, anti-Protestants, anti-clericals, by their mutual provocations, share responsibility for it. The spirit that animates them is neither the Catholic spirit, nor the Jewish spirit, nor the Protestant spirit, but quite simply the spirit of intolerance, nourished by the spirit of war and hatred.

III.

There is, I know, a number of anti-Semites who are indifferent to religious doctrines, who proclaim themselves Free Thinkers, who could be what they say effectively; but they too, if they do not leave religious intolerance at the door, end up fatally at intolerance.

They say: we attack, with respect to the Jew, not religion, but the race, the blood of Israel. Their grievance is purely ethnic.

But how to separate, in the Jew, religion from race? When one calls out for laws of exception against the Jews, when one demands a return to the laws of the Middle Ages or the *ancien régime*, could anyone imagine that such laws would not have any religious character to them? You speak about race; you say: it is race that we are after; but what sign do you recognize it by, this race? If you were dealing with black people, Asians, or Amerindians, that would be easy; there are states, for example, some European colonies where blacks and Asians are struck with certain civil and political incapacities. With the Jews that would not be so easy; for the Jews are, unfortunately, members of the white race just as we are. How would we recognize them? Will it be, really, by the oval of their face, or the curve of their nose? One would greatly risk making an error and mistaking excellent Christians or "Aryans" for Semites. The proof is that in the epochs when there were laws of exception against the Jew, Christians or Muslims invented inflicting distinctive marks on them; it is in this way that they obliged them to wear the small yellow wheel, or the yellow cap, and various external signs of this sort, so that Christians were not exposed to taking this miscreant of a Jew for one of their brothers.

In brief, there is not, with respect to the Jew, a distinctive sign alone, or what amounts to the same thing, between the Christian and him, except for one line of demarcation: religion. The Jew was created by his religion; he has been preserved by it, and if he should come to be detached from it entirely, he would disappear, fatally, insofar as being a Jew. It is the fate, moreover, that seems reserved, if not for everyone, at least for a great number of them. Once again, there is no sure sign of Jewish origin except that of religion. Consequently, any law of exception against the Jews will take on a religious aspect. And, let's be very clear about this, it is the same in every country where there has been laws of exceptions against them, in every country where they still exist. Take ancient Spain for instance, take contemporary Russia, you will find that the laws of exception with respect to the Jews has always had a religious character to it; that the Jews who became Christians were no longer subjected to those laws, or if they continued to be subjected to them, like the Marranos in Spain, it was during a period of transition and because one had serious doubts about the sincerity of their baptism.

Whoever wants then to enact special laws for and against the Jews is driven, whether he likes it or not, to religious persecution. Such is, in sum, the fatal end result of anti-Semitism, and for me, as a Christian and a Frenchman, that alone would suffice to make me condemn it.

As for the Jews, we must believe them when they say that our anti-Semites are upset with them primarily because of their race. We come, therefore, to another grievance, more serious perhaps, because it touches on a greater number of people: the national grievance.

The Jew, it is said, is a foreign element, unassimilable, who denationalizes peoples in whose midst he establishes himself. Terrible reproach in a century like this one when different peoples show themselves to be so strongly and so rightly attached to their nationality. The Jew, it is said, does not want to be French, because the Jew is a Semite, and we others, the French, we are Aryans. There you have it, in its simplicity, the anti-Semites' thesis, and on this simplistic thesis rests all of anti-Semitism. If it has, as they endeavor to boast, a scientific basis, it is right there; they would be unable to point to another. Now, is it true that the Jew is a pure Semite, and that we others, Christians originally, are all Aryans? – Many among us know that what one took for races for so long a time was not, most of the time, but groups of peoples, and that what one called Semitic races and Aryan races would have been more correctly denominated Semitic languages and Aryan languages.

Anti-Semitism's fundamental error is that of being based on the idea of race, of attributing an inordinate value to that idea of race and to the opposition between Aryan and Semite. He forgets that with respect to race itself, insomuch as race, just as with respect to its origins, its elements, and its aptitudes, we know very little ordinarily, and that instead of being fixed and unchanging, race constantly changes, throughout the centuries, from an intellectual point of view primarily, according to chance crossbreeding or according to the influence of events and milieus.

We have writers, journalists, proud of a thin veneer of erudition, who go repeating, each morning, that the battle waged by anti-Semitism is nothing but the continuation of the long battles of Rome against Carthage, of Scipio against Hannibal, of Charles Martel against the Spanish Arabs, of the Crusaders against Saladin, and so forth. It is an already debunked philosophy of history. It is difficult to take that practically irreducible antagonism between the Aryan and the Semite seriously, when if one kept only to the facts there is so little opposition, one could say so little difference, between the Aryan and the Semite that it is often difficult to distinguish between them. Then also we know that, today, if our languages are Aryan, the background of our French and European populations is probably not Aryan.

I do not wish to expatiate here on those fastidious questions of ethnology, but I am forced to examine the anti-Semite's line of reasoning in his theory on race: he will tell you that one must be on one's guard against this Semitic race, that one must keep it at a distance because it is a race that tends to corrupt others and subjugate them at one and the same time. In anti-Semitic anthropology or ethnology, the Aryans, that is to say those who are not Jews, possess all the qualities, all the virtues, generosity notably; they alone understand the sentiment of honor. The Semite, contrariwise, has all the shortcomings, all the vices, all the baseness. He is a vile being, whereas the Aryan is a noble being, – an antithesis to which is easy to develop and I would amuse myself in doing so. To the one, to the Aryan, – our German neighbors say to the German, – everything that is generous, ideal, elevated in our civilization; to the other, to the Semite, all that is covered by sordid passions and material instincts.[21] The anti-Semites forget one thing, however, which is that if the Semitic peoples or the Semitic language has played a role in the world, it has played it primarily through religion, by the monotheism of Israel, and by Christianity, which has its origins in Israel.

The Semitic race, the Jewish race, particularly, if it is an inferior race, mercantile, devoid of the ideal, how to explain that from it has originated the trunk of all the great religions? How can a Christian, notably, consider the blood of Israel as an impure blood, or as an ignoble blood, when the founder of Christianity issued from that blood of Israel, as well as his mother, and his disciples, and the apostles who brought the Christian faith to the world?

Even in this regard, I would dare say that not only is anti-Semitism not scientifically based, that it opposes all notions of contemporary science, but that it is in opposition to the history and traditions of Christianity, as well as with the spirit of the Gospel.

Let us take contemporary Jews; they make up, so the argument goes, a race of people isolated from those among whom they live. If that is true, in certain countries predominately, it is true because, first of all, the Jew is isolated by his religion; and in this regard, the fact of the Jew's isolation is not so singular as first

---

[21]Original footnote: Such is, in our infantile simplicity, the thesis put forward recently even, by a writer of English origin, the admirer and commentator of Wagner, M. Houston Steward Chamberlain, in a work published in German: *Die Grundlagen des neunzehnten Jahrhunderts* (Munich, Brachmann, 2 vol.).

meets the eye. If you look at the Middle East, you will see populations that are in an analogous situation to that of the Jew, ancient peoples who, they too, have been in some way embalmed and preserved, throughout the centuries, in their Church; such as the Armenian, the Copt, the Greek himself for a long time.

There is then in this a phenomenon that is not particular to the Jew. For him, as for the Copt, as for the Armenian or the Parsi, both of which are associated by ethnologists with the Aryan trunk, what one is led to attribute to race is most often the fact of history or persecution. Israel, I can never grow tired saying it, is much less the fruit of race than the work of history. Two things, above all, have made the Jew and given to him, under all latitudes, a particular aspect: secular isolation and traditional ritual.[22]

In terms of defects and qualities, the Jew is explained less by his ethnic origins and by his parentage with old Semites than by the multiple and grievous peripeteias of his more than thirty times secular history. The modern Jew, primarily, has been formed, has been fashioned by a thousand years of persecutions, by laws of exception, by isolation and seclusion in the ghetto. He carries, into his recent liberation even, the mark of the chains of his long servitude. It is one of the things that, for me, gives so much interest to the study of the Jews. The philosopher, the politician, the sociologist, not to mention the naturalist, learn from it how history can form and also deform man; how it can model and sculpt, in some way, a human group, adding to or subtracting from his

---

[22]Original footnote: See *Israel Among Nations* (chap. XIII).

work without cease. If there is a Jewish race, it is, I dare say, the artificial product of the Mosaic law and of our laws from the Middle Ages, it is the work of the Torah and of the ghetto, much more than the natural product of the soil or of a climate, or the spontaneous fruit of the Semitic trunk and the blood of the patriarchs. No race perhaps is more manifestly the result of historic evolution.

Also, in order to understand the Jew, in order to make sense of his "psychology" as well as his "physiology" or his "pathology," one must always go back to the history of Israel, – to its history, above all since the fall of the Temple and the dispersion.

Nowhere does the past better explain the present. Thus is it for almost all the physical or moral traits attributed to contemporary Jews, as individuals, and as an ethnic group. Thus is it notably for one of the principal reproaches made by anti-Semites with respect to the clan spirit, to the tribal spirit.

That tribal spirit has been maintained for a long time among the Jews; many among them, in the Middle East at least, have not yet freed themselves from it. But, this tribal spirit, whence does it come? Is it unique to the Jew? It comes, in part, from his law, the Mosaic law that he has preserved, which constrains him to complicated practices; it comes from Talmudic precepts that, after the dispersion of Israel, in order to prevent its dissolution amidst the mass of pagan peoples, they girded so to speak with a protective hedge of observances of every sort.

But is this the only reason for the clan spirit

attributed to the Jews? If the Jews, over the centuries, have lived in our cities, enclosed in the walls of a distinct quarter, has it always been them who obstinately isolated themselves from other inhabitants of the country? When the ghetto closed its gates each evening, was it solely by the order or under the inspiration of its rabbis? Did the laws of Christian peoples not have any hand in it? Do we want to be just and respect history, then we must recognize that if the tribal spirit of the Jews has been, in part, fomented by themselves, by their cult, by their rabbis, it was also, even more, over the centuries, fomented by the laws of the peoples in whose midst they lived, by the restrictions that our ancestors put on their freedom. Today even, as you know, there are countries in which the Jews are corralled into certain areas; in Russia, for example, they cannot leave what one calls the territory open to the Jews; in certain cities of the Middle East, they remain confined in a quarter where it is forbidden them to escape. Is it, today, the Jews who persist to keep themselves at a distance from other inhabitants of the country? No, certainly not; they are, the most often, constrained, against their will. If one still finds, in our days, traces of that ancient tribal spirit, the responsibility falls, primarily, on the laws that had condemned the Israelites to a prolonged isolation.

I will even go further; it is a reflection that I have often heard made to anti-Semites, regarding worldly relations: these Jews, they said, are said to impose themselves on us; they want to force us to mix with them. But if the Jews want to mix with us that proves that they do not want to isolate themselves from us. We dare to put forward that if one meets, today even, a spirit of isolation and desire for separation between Christians and Jews, it comes more from the Christians than from the Jews.

The clan spirit, the tribal spirit, always alive among the Jews, push them, it is said, to an excessive confraternity and solidarity of race, at the same time as it makes them strangers to the interests and patriotism of the people among whom they live. Today, as in the Middle Ages, the Jews camped in the middle of Christian nations would not know any other compatriots than Jews, their brethren. They have not, like us, taken root in the soil of the country where they live; they are morally strangers there; they remain a cosmopolite everywhere, and to be quite honest "without a country."

If there is any foundation to this reproach, the fault is still with their history in the past, with anti-Semitism in the present. Jewish solidarity, too vaunted at times perhaps, this solidarity that Christians sometimes could take for their model, has been fortified by secular persecutions, and at the moment when freedom and equality of rights began to loosen the bonds, the menaces of anti-Semitism have returned to tighten them again and consolidate them.

One could say the same thing about patriotism. In all the countries where they had been emancipated, the Jews allowed themselves to go, joyously, with the natural feeling of love for their birth country. They were proud to become citizens and made themselves the honor of fulfilling their duties. Anti-

Semitism came along to contest them that right; it pointed out to them, with a gesture, the pathways of exile; in many countries, it has constrained them, by dint of vexations, to seek a new abode, in less intolerant lands. If one has seen the Jews of Austria or the Middle East preaching Zionism, engaging their coreligionists to create for themselves again, in Palestine, a Jewish fatherland, together with a Jewish State, it is because the furies of anti-Semitism have made them despair of being otherwise able to possess a fatherland and of ever being regarded, by Christians, as compatriots.

Zionism is merely the consequence of anti-Semitic exclusivism. It presented itself like a port of refuge to the Jews of Romania and the Middle East, whose laws or mores refused them a fatherland in the land of their birth. But, everywhere else, in all the countries where they have been admitted to the rights of citizens, the Jews have been too attached to the hospitable land that had welcomed them than to seek out another fatherland, on the banks of the biblical Jordan even.

In states that have granted them equality and the rights of citizens, there primarily where they have been allowed to take part in public affairs, in Germany, in England, in Italy, in France even, I do not believe that the Jews have shown themselves to be less good patriots than their fellow Christian citizens, or that one could point out a particularly Jewish politics, uniquely inspired by the interests of Israel, among them.

Among those people of Jewish origin who

have arrived at the heights of power, Disraeli, Lord Beaconsfield is without a doubt he who has climbed the highest. If he retained, in his person and in his predilections, a trace of his Israelite origins, the noble lord, who was the first patron of British imperialism, was no less devoted to the greatness of England. If he has shown himself in certain aspects to be inferior to his great rival, Gladstone, it is certainly not because of his patriotism.

The Jews have been able to give witness not only to their affection for the country that had emancipated them, to the states that gave them access to freedom, they have also often given witness to their love for oppressed countries, where freedom of rights had been refused to them, such as Poland or Italy recently.

It is not in Italy that one would be well received to reproach Israelites for a lack of patriotism. Many, like M. L. Luzzatti, have been among the first champions of the *Risorgimento* and of Italian unity. Among the names that have remained particularly dear to Italian patriots shines that of the a man whose tomb Italy placed under the porticoes of Saint Mark's Basilica in Venice, Daniel Manin. Manin, who, in the darkest hours of the revolution of 1848, fought alone, for weeks, for Venice and against the Austrian armies, he was, as one knows, of Jewish origin. He is yet another example to oppose to the pamphleteers who teach that all the Jews and sons of Jews are cosmopolites and without a fatherland. The truth is that, when one takes Europe, when one takes America as an example, the Jew is attached to his fatherland, in all the states where the laws and the customs permit him to have a fatherland; and in more than one country, as in Italy or in Hungary, he has contributed, by the sweat of his brow and by his blood, to the enfranchisement of that country. If one wanted to identify which particular nuances this noble sentiment of patriotism takes in the contemporary Jew's soul, one could say, together with a recent historian,[23] that if it is often of recent date, like their emancipation itself, "if it does not yet depend on a long heredity, or on a simple and naïve feeing for the soil, patriotism among the Jews draws its source from inspirations based on reason and is born of the grateful transports of the heart." Consequently, also, in a correct observation by the same historian, Jewish patriotism, far from being necessarily less pure and less elevated than our own, is more easily detached from all the so-called nationalistic prejudices, "from all those hatreds imbibed with one's mother's milk," that too often vitiate the patriotism of the mass of people and transform it into an inept Chauvinism or into a narrow nationalism.

As for the reproach so often addressed at the Jews, of everywhere forming a State within the State, it is one of the grievances that we encounter among the three "anti"; we might examine it, as well, with respect to the Protestants, with respect to the Catholics. To form a State within the State is an old accusation that has been particularly abused, which parties or religious groups enjoy hurling at each other and which they would do better to let it slide because

[23]Original footnote: M. Théodore Reinach, *History of the Israelites since the Fall of the Jewish State* (Hachette, 2nd edition, 1901).

it can be invoked against each of them. If one were to believe the three "anti," there would be so many States within the State today that the danger would be greatly diminished, so much so that these States within the State are at war with each other. This is moreover a point on which we will have to return. I would not go so far as to say, myself, that modern states are so fragile, or that contemporary nations so weak, that it would be difficult for them to resist the Israelite cosmopolitanism, Protestant cosmopolitanism, or even Catholic cosmopolitanism.

IV.

We arrive now at the grievance that touches perhaps the greatest number of our fellow citizens, the economic grievance, the social grievance. We are told that the Jews are not only a race of foreign origin, they are a race of parasites; they willingly practice professions where one lives at the expense of another.

That reproach is heard everywhere, I have no need to insist on it; it is so well known. The Semite is a parasitic race. It is his vocation. If this is true of the Semite, there are, on earth, other parasitic races; there are, in the Middle East, for example, populations of Christians who, for similar reasons, find themselves in a situation analogous to that of the Jews. Take the unfortunate Armenians whom the Sultan's policies have undertaken to exterminate, and whose massacre Christian Europe has left unpunished. When the Muslims cut the throat of the Armenians of Trebizond and of Istanbul, among whom more than one moneylender was found, the debtors who went to settle their debts by suppressing their creditors also treated them like parasites. They applied the principles of anti-Semitism to the Armenians.

A parasitic race! It is a terrible reproach, in the current day. Let's reflect for a moment on the meaning of this word. If the Jew is a parasite, is he the only parasite in our society? We are not aware of other groups, other parties besides the anti-Semites, who today use, they too, this reproach of parasitism? Do we not know that it is leveled against others besides Israelites? Have we never heard it resonating in our ears before? To believe certain of our contemporaries and compatriots, we would be, nearly all of us, today, parasites, because all those who do not live by the labor of their hands, by the sweat of their brow, in the Biblical expression, would be, according to new theories, parasites. Now, this sort of parasitism which is leveled by the anti-Semites against the Jews is, it must be said, identical to the same grievance leveled by socialists against the bourgeois.

Can one treat as parasites men who live by liberal professions, or even those who give themselves to industry, or even commerce? If that is the case, then there would be quite a large number of other parasites besides the Jews, and as business, commerce, and banks play an ever more important role in our contemporary societies, it would turn out that our societies would have become ever more parasitic. Do we need to remember that this is what the socialists maintain?

I do not need to demonstrate the inanity of this

thesis; I will permit myself only to state that, in this respect, the accusation of anti-Semites against the Jews is the same as that of the socialists leveled against the bourgeois. It is true, or it seems to be true, – for in order to fully elucidate this matter one must needs have the leisure to examine it in detail in each country, in each city almost. It seems true that by their numbers one finds among the Jews a greater proportion of men who turn to business, commerce, finance. These professions, despite everything, are necessary, they are indispensable; it would be unfortunate to see too great a number of men dedicated to them, but if, in our democracy, one feared, in this respect, an imbalance, the fault would not be with the Jews. They are far from being the only ones to escape manual labor, or the only ones to want to conduct business. As we will soon see, the principal grievance against them is that they succeeded perhaps better than others.

But why do the Jews gravitate towards business? And why do many of them succeed? History explains this to us. Why do they take to finance most notably? It is because the past groomed them for this profession, and not only the past groomed them, but the religious laws or civil laws of peoples in whose midst they lived constrained them and confined them to it, throughout the centuries. Has one forgotten that the laws of the *ancien régime* forbid them from practicing any other profession?

It is said that many Jews work in the banking sector, just as many are moneychangers; contrary to popular prejudices, the number of Jewish bankers and financiers is infinitely less than supposed by the anti-Semites in France notably. No matter: for a long time formerly, finance and moneychanging were the monopoly of the Jews, and it was a monopoly that had been imposed on them.

It is Aryans or Christians who, to some degree, had imposed this monopoly on them by our laws. For centuries, the laws of Christian peoples interdicted, under the vague name of usury, the commerce of money, the borrowing of money by Christians; and because it was necessary that this business of money was handled by *someone*, it was abandoned to the Jews. It is in this way that we ourselves have, laboriously and artificially, for generations, developed in the Jews these financial and commercial faculties that many among us today come to reproach them for. They seek, as you know, to wriggle out of it, and to level subsequently another reproach: "How's that!? It is not enough for you to monopolize finance, to take the upper hand in commerce, now you want to invade our other professions!... No, that is intolerable, go back to your money counter." – And, in effect, it happens that in Europe, as in France even, a large number of Israelites who had tried to live by other professions, who had studied for other careers, who had begun to succeed in them, were obliged to abandon them and to return, in spite of themselves, to the business of money and their father's counter. Here, still, the case of the Jews is not so particular as the anti-Semites imagine it; their history is that of other groups, that of peoples isolated by their religion, which I mentioned earlier, such as the Greeks, the Armenians, the Copts, the Parsi, certain

Syrians. But is it really true that, among us, all of commerce, all of finance is in the hands of the Israelites? Is it true that, with the aid of that secular and forced education which was given to them by the Middle Ages and by the *ancien régime*, they have become so superior that we are incapable of competing with them?

If one examines the facts, it is impossible to deny that the so-called financial supremacy of the Jews has been inordinately exaggerated. If one counts the number of great banking houses in France, for example, we would find that there are very few Israelite ones. The high bank, today, in France, is for the most part in Christian hands, – a good part of which is in Protestant hands; and it is a reproach that one makes sometimes of the Protestants, as if to excel in a profession were a burden or a crime. If it ever possessed it, the high bank of the Jews has lost the preponderance attributed to it over the Stock Exchange and the French financial markets. It is, at minimum, an anachronism to speak to us, with the anti-Semites or with the socialists, about Jewish financial feudality.[24]

[24]Original footnote: On this point, the anti-Semites and the socialists, by denouncing credit companies, often commit the same error. One will allow me to cite, in this note, several lines by my brother Paul Leroy-Beaulieu (*The French Economist*, April 13, 1901), with respect to attacks by M. Viviani in the *La Lanterne* newspaper against the "two billions" of credit companies, represented by the socialist deputy as an instrument of "M. Rothschild."

"This proposition, which makes of credit companies the subsidiaries in some sort, or the associates or the servants of M. Rothschild, is the most surprising possible. Everyone knows, on the contrary, that credit companies are the competitors and, what is more, the happy and growing competitors, of the great house

And, if we look outside France, we see that there are other countries – and precisely the richest, where the situation of the Jews is less than with us; where among the very great fortunes it is not found to be in the hands of those Semites, as represented by our anti-Jews, like natural kings, if not like the legitimate kings of money.

One has put together, in England and in the

---

of rue Laffitte as much as of the Bank of France itself. We do not wish to say anything negative about the celebrated family bank that deserves respect by its faithfulness to traditions and to the work ethic; but it is absolutely certain that the situation of this house was much more preponderant under the Restoration, under the reign of Louis-Phillippe and in the first part of the French Second Empire, than it is today.

"Credit companies were born beside it, outside it, without it and in part against it. These companies are considerably large, their clientele grows, their powers of placement and projection grow as well. They have particularly represented the rise of financial democracy, with respect to the ancient houses, what was formerly called the high bank. This latter is confined today to several enterprises, several insurance companies, several old businesses. The entire personnel of the credit companies is a relatively new personnel; to look at the names of the men who are at the head of these institutions, one does not find any that are of any great renown, for half a century; the great banking houses from the end of the 18th century and the first half of the 19th still have, many do at any rate, active and honored representatives, just like the famous house of rue Laffitte. But the principal financial organs, those that have the vastest clientele, the most decisive influence, are in the hands of new faces.

"And it is like this, not only for the credit companies, but for all the new publicly-traded companies; if one studies them, if one looks at them closely for the last quarter of a century or half a century even, one will see that they have, almost all, new men at their head, men whose names do not figure among the senior administration of finance under the reign of Louis-Phillippe.

United States, comparative tables of great fortunes; among the fifteen or twenty great fortunes of England there are only one or two Israelite ones; and of the twelve or fifteen great American fortunes, not one is Jewish. In England, as in the United States, the Jews however are free to choose their career; they are very numerous, and they have complete freedom. I remember, in this regard, a curious phrase that deserves being cited. Several years ago, in the sister city of New York, Brooklyn (today annexed to the city of New York) inaugurated an Israelite hospital, constructed with Israelite funds. The mayor of Brooklyn, who was present at the opening of this hospital, gave a speech in which he boasted the qualities of the Jews: "But," he said while finishing up, "do not be too proud; you think perhaps that you are the kings of commerce, the kings of the dollar? Not at all, you are but children next to us; as far as *making money* is concerned, there is nobody but the Yankee."

It is necessary to examine the reproach made so often against the Jews of being too rich; one might say that, except for a few, they are all millionaires, according to certain newspapers, almost all billionaires? If we consider the bulk of the Jews in the contemporary world we will discover, on the contrary, that they are very poor; I believe that there is not, on our planet, a race more pray to such a pauperism. If one wishes to form one's own judgment, one needs to travel to Poland and to Russia. In Paris even, there are

---

"We know of no more convincing proof than this that the situation of modern companies do not involve any financial feudality, that is, any prolonged hereditary transmission of prepotency in finance or industry."

streets where a rather dense population of Jews live, and that population is poor. If you go to London, and you are curious to visit the quarters of East End, Whitechapel, where the mean people are piled up on each other in mean hovels (notwithstanding serious progress that has been made in this area in recent years), you will find that the population of the most unsanitary and miserable slums of London is, in large part, Israelite.

There is even in London and in New York an anti-Semitism of a particular kind. What reproach do the English and the Americans make against the Israelites? They say: the Jewish proletarian (for there is a true proletarian, in the etymological sense, as in the economic sense of the word), by his poverty, by his work faculty, by his endurance, by his sobriety, tends to lower the wages of workers. And in order to oppose this lowering of wages by the manual labor of Israelites, Americans and English have asked that the law prevent the debarkation of immigrants without resources. In certain professions, in fact, those in which the labor is the most poorly remunerated, in seamstering, in the tailoring or cobbler professions, a large number of workers are Jewish; in London, as in New York, they are the principal victims of that mode of exploitation justly damned by the name of *sweating system*.

If the mass of Jews has remained poor and impoverished, it is no less true that some among them have attained a great fortune, several thousands of them in possession of an easy life, and that suffices to attract much envy to them. One does not wish to see,

among the Jews, anything but the elite arrive at
wealth or success. In an epoch when numbers are everything, or pretend to be everything, the Jews show
that numbers are not everything; it is perhaps one of
the things that one pardons them the least for. The
Jew, it is said, takes more than his fair share. We will
see, with respect to the Protestants, against whom the
same reproach is made, to just what degree that grievance is founded. What irritates us, in a like case,
against the Jews, is just how often they attain success,
and consequently even, the qualities that permit them
to obtain success. One often says that these victories
in financial struggles are owing to their lack of scruples, but one does not owe durable victories to bad
faith or fraud. No, if the Jews succeed in business affairs, if they have made a way for themselves in so
many diverse careers, it is because of their qualities,
because of their spirit of initiative, because of their
patience, their energy, their suppleness or flexibility,
their perseverance. These are the most common qualities among them; they are what they owe their suc-
cesses to; and instead of reproaching such qualities in
them, we ourselves would do better to acquire them
and practice them, with as much energy.

I heard, for example, not too long ago, the
mother of a family, speaking about a secondary
school in Paris where her son was enrolled, exclaim:
"The Jews are always first; they take all the prizes;
it's intolerable!" Do we really find in that a motive
for exclusion? Will we really chase from France a
group that has too many intelligent children, too
many intelligent young people? I confess that it is not
in this way that I understand patriotism. I will go even

further: I am deeply humiliated when I bump into such compatriots as these, who seem to think themselves incapable of competing against those whom they call, contemptuously, the Semites. As for myself, as a Frenchman of old stock, as an Aryan, to use the term that is dear to anti-Semites, I do not feel such humility. It could have happened to me as well, at secondary school, or elsewhere, to compete against "Semites"; but, however redoubtable they might have been, I was not afraid to compete with them; and for me, for my friends and family, in all conflicts of competition, I claim no privilege; I do not claim anything but freedom and equality.

When we examine the reproaches addressed by anti-Semites against what they call Jewish capitalism, one thing strikes us; it is that anti-Semitism results in a sort of anti-capitalism, and consequently in a sort of socialism. On this terrain, the anti-Semites give a hand to the socialists; they come to the same conclusion, with this difference that the socialists, more logical, direct their attacks on capitalism at all capitalists, whereas the illogicalness of the anti-Semites makes them direct their anger only at the Jews, at the Protestants whom they regard as half-Jews, or at those Catholics whom they designate by the particularly elastic name of Judaizers.

Anti-Semitism results in this way in socialism, right-leaning socialism if you like, so-called conservative socialism; but illogical socialism, bastardized socialism, socialism without an ideal, socialism which is not even nimbused with an aureole of fraternity.

This anti-Semitic socialism is that of men who have not succeeded in their business affairs; it is also that of certain social categories; it is, for example, the socialism of a proprietor who has seen his revenues decrease, or who compares his situation to that of the great merchants, the great industrialists, the great financiers. It is a kind of provincial and rural socialism; it is also, as I have already remarked, but it is good to repeat it, a socialism of the salon, a socialism of the chateau, a socialism of white gloves, a socialism of country squires and dowagers. For men discontented with their destiny, for those who find that fortune has not responded to their hopes, for those whose revenues are inferior to their appetites, it is precious to have, as a living target, a restrained group on which one can direct, with its rancors and its envies, the anger of the masses.

It is what, in the eyes of many good folks, gives the advantage to anti-Semitism over socialism. Socialism is compromising, it is perilous; anti-Semitism is not at all, or it does not seem to be. Socialism singles out the "bourgeois" for peoples' envy and hatred. By "bourgeois" they mean whatever is bad, it is a vague and imprecise term; the bourgeois, one does not know where that begins or ends; to attack the bourgeois can be dangerous for ourselves; the Jew, on the other hand, is a type of caste; it is a defined group, one can point it out with impunity, for the anger of the populace. Perhaps one would do well not to trust in it overly much. Anti-Semitism calls for the revision of fortunes, sometimes by law, sometimes by pillage; this revision of fortunes, which is effected in one manner or another, can be perilous for others besides the Jews. That day when the treasury or the populace wants to undertake it, I fear that neither the treasury nor the chaos would respectfully stop before Christian houses. In Russia, in Romania, at the time of the disorders against the Jews, Christians hastened to hang holy icons on their doors in order to protect themselves before the coming violence; if the hateful predications of anti-Semites must forever raise popular fury among us, I strongly doubt, in order to preserve ourselves against it, that it suffices for Christians to mark their houses with a cross, or to put their shops under the protection of the Virgin.

V.

It is time to conclude. In supposing that their grievances were founded, is there any means of giving satisfaction to the anti-Semites? I confess, for my own part, that I do not see any. What to do with the Jews? Act against them as the Sultan-Caliph did towards the Armenians, exterminating them, by iron or by fire, raising against them fanaticism or the anger of the mob? It is the same solution that the energumens of anti-Semitism push towards, unconsciously perhaps; but, as exalted as their hatred is, the majority of our anti-Jews are too humane to dare to recommend such a bloody method; they feel that while it has remained a procedure of Middle Eastern politics, massacre is no longer a recourse for French politics. What to do with the Jews then? Exile them? But where to send them? Let us not forget that the anti-Semites want to banish them from every country simultaneously; the means is radical, but it is not practical.

But there is actually a solution preconized by certain Jews, who are directly under the menace of anti-Semitism, and it is what one calls Zionism, it is the reconstitution of an Israel state. Zionism is an idea from the Middle Ages, an old dream from the ancient ghettoes, which seemed dead with the emancipation of the Jews; if it has reconquered adherents among the Jews, it owes it, as I have just now said, to the menaces of anti-Semitism. But can one find a solution? Palestine, Syria even, is too small or too poor to sustain ten million Israelites as they are numbered today; then again, supposing a Jewish state in Palestine, do you suppose that the Christians would consent to abandon their holy places to the care of Israel? And will all the Jews want to be relocated to the Holy Land? Ask the Jews who live in France, those who were born here, who were raised here; they will tell you that they find themselves quite nicely in France, that France is their country, and that they wish to remain here; so this is no solution then.

There is only one solution; it is the common law, it is freedom. We find ourselves faced with this alternative, either the stake or freedom; I confess, as for myself, I resolutely opt for freedom.

A last comment, which I allow myself to offer to you for your consideration. I have often asked myself what would have changed for us if there had not been any Jews in France. Ask yourself, each one of you, this question: reflect on it, in good conscience; what would have changed, amongst us, if all the Jews of France had been expelled or burned by the anti-

Semites of the past? I have often thought about it, and here is what my reflections have led me to: nothing, nothing would have changed, or almost nothing, in France. We would have lost some men of high distinction, scientists, philologists, for example, like M. Bréal and M. Oppert, physicians like M. Lippmann, poets like M. Eugène Manuel, artists like Sarah Bernhardt, and I could cite other names, nothing but those from among the living. There would have been here and there changes in person; one would see a few less exotic names on the signboards along the boulevards, and a few more Christians standing under the porticoes of the Stock Exchange; but, outside of that, what would have changed? As much as I try, I cannot find a thing.

How could nothing have changed? The anti-Semites will cry: do you not see that France is in the process of becoming Jewish!... But, that's just it, I do not see it; as wide as I open my eyes, I do not see the Judaization of France and Europe. What do you mean by the Judaization of our societies? You mean, doubtless, the predominance of material interests, the preponderance of industry, commerce, finance; you mean the reign of money, the tyranny of gold. By admitting, with the anti-Semite, that money is king and tyrant of our epoch, I do not see, in truth, what is particularly Jewish about that. That is no more conformant with the Israelite spirit than the Christian one. That prepotency of money, which cynics exaggerate perhaps, – for everything is not yet for sale in our country of France, – that royalty of money that rightfully shocks our *delicatesse*, where does it come from? It comes from all the conditions of modern life,

it comes first of all from our French Revolution; it results from the destruction of all privileges; it origi-
nates from the fact that, in our contemporary society,
the soil has been systematically leveled. There no
longer remains hardly, among men and families, but
one distinction, that of fortune, having become moreover accessible to everyone, according to each person's talents and chances. What is there in this that is
particularly Jewish, specifically Semitic? It is a social
phenomenon that is explained by the ensemble of our
political and economical conditions, and which would
persist even when we no longer had a single Jew living in France.[25]

Do we want to emancipate our contemporary
societies from this excessive predominance of material interests; do we want to free ourselves from the
preponderance or the tyranny of money; we do not
need to chase away the Jews; we need to do a particularly more urgent and more difficult thing, – reform
our hearts, our feelings, our ideas, our behaviors. We
need to relearn the taste for simplicity and to free ourselves from the servitude of luxury or the excessive
needs for well-being. And, Jewish or Christian, we
can hardly do that except by returning to the message
of the Bible and to the message contained in the
Gospel which, on this point, as on so many other
points, is inspired in reality by the same principles.[26]

---

[25]Original footnote: See, on this topic, a series of articles
published by us in the *Revue des Deux Mondes*, in 1897 and
1898, under the title of "The Reign of Money."

[26]Original footnote: If, among the solutions proposed by anti-
Semites, the laws of exception are not mentioned here, it is a
point that we examine later on in our Conclusion, by treating

---

simultaneously of the measures of the sort claimed by anti-Semites and by anti-clericals. When laws against the Jews are similar to laws of exception in the *ancien régime*, inapplicable to modern France, the example of Russia, where they are still in use, would suffice to demonstrate their disadvantages and ineffectiveness. – See *Empire of the Tsars and the Russians*, tome III, book IV, chapter 11.

Other Books by the Publisher

Fanchette's Pretty Little Foot by Restif de La Bretonne

Je M'Accuse... by Léon Bloy

My Hospitals & My Prisons by Paul Verlaine

Salvation Through the Jews by Léon Bloy

Words of a Demolitions Contractor by Léon Bloy

Cellulely by Paul Verlaine

Ecclesiastical Laurels by Jacques Rochette de la Morlière

Flowers of Bitumen by Émile Goudeau

Songs for Her & Odes in Her Honor by Paul Verlaine

On Huysmans' Tomb by Léon Bloy

Ten Years a Bohemian by Émile Goudeau

The Soul of Napoleon by Léon Bloy

Blood of the Poor by Léon Bloy

Joan of Arc and Germany by Léon Bloy

A Platonic Love by Paul Alexis

The Revealer of the Globe: Christopher Columbus & His Future Beatification (Part One) by Léon Bloy

Poems Saturnian by Paul Verlaine

The Biography of Léon Bloy: Memories of a Friend by René Martineau

Fredegund, France: A Book of Poetry by Richard Robinson

The Good Song by Paul Verlaine

Swans by Francis Vielé-Griffin

Constantinople and Byzantium by Léon Bloy

Enamels and Cameos by Théophile Gautier

Four Years of Captivity in Cochons-sur-Marne: 1900-1904 by Léon Bloy

Dark Minerva: Prolegomena: The Moral Construction of Dante's Divine Comedy by Giovanni Pascoli

What is Fascism: Discourses and Polemics by Giovanni Gentile

The Desperate Man by Léon Bloy

Meditations of a Solitary in 1916 by Léon Bloy

The Ride of Yeldis & Other Poems by Francis Vielé-Griffin

Silvie & The Chimeras by Gérard de Nerval

Italian Nationalism by Enrico Corradini

A Silver-Grey Death and *Drowning* by Yu Dafu

www.ingramcontent.com/pod-product-compliance
Lightning Source LLC
Chambersburg PA
CBHW031421120626
46545CB00006B/2223